Film as Film

Film as Film

Understanding and Judging Movies

V. F. Perkins

New introduction by Foster Hirsch

DA CAPO PRESS

Library of Congress Cataloging in Publication Data

Perkins, V. F., 1936–
   Film as film: understanding and judging movies / V. F. Perkins; with
new introduction by Foster Hirsch.—1st Da Capo ed.
     p.   cm.
   Originally published: New York: Penguin Books, 1972.
   Includes index.
   ISBN 0-306-80541-3
   1. Motion pictures. I. Title.
PN1994.P394   1993   93-25278
781.43'015—dc20   CIP

First Da Capo Press edition 1993

This Da Capo Press edition of *Film As Film*, supplemented with a
new introduction by Foster Hirsch, is an unabridged republication
of the edition published in London in 1991. It is reprinted by
arrangement with Viking Penguin.

4   5   6   7   8   9   10

Published by Da Capo Press
A Member of the Perseus Books Group
http://www.dacapopress.com

Manufactured in the United States of America

Introduction to the Da Capo Edition

Why is the jeep scene in *Carmen Jones*, as directed by Otto Preminger, a truer use of film than the sequence in *Battleship Potemkin* in which stone lions appear to rise up from their pedestals? In *Film as Film*, V.F. Perkins argues that in *Carmen Jones* cutting and framing underscore the conflicts that divide the two characters in the scene, whereas in *Battleship Potemkin* Eisenstein's use of the lions is an implanted device that showcases the director's bravura staccato editing at the expense of thematic coherence. Preminger's style is seamless, Eisenstein's is declamatory, and in favoring the former Perkins is speaking up for the kind of artistic choice that seeks invisibility. "Synthesis . . . where there is no distinction between how and what, content and form, is what interests us if we are interested in film as film," he suggests.

Perkins' style is as unobtrusive and as alight with a commonsensical use of his own medium as the jeep scene in *Carmen Jones*. First published in 1972, *Film as Film* confronts the large, perennial questions of theory in a language of refreshing clarity, directness, and simplicity. Written before the French heavy-hitters had inundated the academic marketplace, here is film theory cleansed of jargon and making no attempt to be intellectually hip. It is, frankly, a relief to encounter a sophisticated theoretical argument that contains no reference to any French author except André Bazin; that does not invoke the latest buzz words of the semioticians, deconstructionists, post-modernists, linguists, Marxists, psychoanalysts, militant feminists, and multiculturalists; that is innocent of the contributions to intellectual debate of Barthes, Bataille, Baudrillard, Foucault, Derrida,

Lacan, Mulvey, Kristeva, Heath, Levi-Strauss, Irigaray, Metz, Baudry, Mitry, Saussure, Comolli, Althusser. The concepts that have permeated the academic approach to film over the last two decades have yielded many valuable insights—but at a cost. Too often the points worth savoring are embedded in a daunting, punishing style. Impenetrability has been raised to a criterion of value, and zapped by the latest goods from the continent many American (and British) academics have transformed the study of film into a discourse of exclusion, written by and for hard-core specialists.

By and large academics seduced by French imports haven't expressed themselves with the sex appeal that invigorates the best of their models, Roland Barthes most of all. Barthes is an original, succulent thinker whose writing attains a music all its own, but the faux-Barthesian mode he has unwittingly inspired has often been a quest for forbidding, arcane diction that seems designed to repel most student (as well as faculty) comprehension. Now here is Perkins, who was in the field before the crusaders, and focusing on many of the same issues, but in a limpid style that promotes rather than silences dialogue; his book abounds with suggestions for further debate. Read again twenty years later, Perkins provides a return to first causes—to the founding principles of theory. Instead of the spiky armor of the up-to-the-minute reports from the front, Perkins uses such plain, old-fashioned terminology as balance, coherence, credibility, significance, satisfaction, meaning, form, and content. He writes of a film's story world rather than its diegesis; of the activities of seeing and hearing rather than of scopic regimes and invocatory drives; of interpretation rather than hermeneutics; and, rather than wading into the intricacies of suture, of how an audience is persuaded to identify with characters and actions. There is, however, one area in which time has caught up with him—he ignores gendered spectatorship, and a sentence such as "film has been equipped to capture more aspects of reality . . . so that the man in front of the screen comes ever nearer to seeing as much and as clearly as the man beside the camera," is likely to elicit a gasp or a groan from many contemporary readers.

If Perkins is not difficult, he isn't a racy, mass-market populist either. He's an exacting critic whose voice of British reserve nonetheless contains ripe turns of phrase and whose classical symmetries and antitheses often achieve aphoristic thrust. Here are some examples of the kind of syntactical victories Perkins' unassuming style often claims: "Criticism and its theory are concerned with the interplay of available resources and desirable functions. They attempt to establish what the medium is good for. They cannot determine what is good for the medium, because the question is senseless." "Film reviewers have made us familiar with the notion that a director can transcend the limitations of a genre; quite often in movies we see genre transcending the limitations of the director."

Despite his good manners, like all true theorists Perkins is stumping for a cause. Instead of the "either/or" of most theoretical debate, however, he proposes "and." Citing film's "peculiarly mixed parentage," its "inherent impurity," he wants to expand our understanding of the medium's possibilities. He distances himself from the die-hard formalists and realists—he shuns the notion of "pure" film and dismisses any search for the "essence" of film—to offer a theoretical model that embraces the medium's heterogeneity, its use of both realism and magic, its ability to record as well as to create. "Synthesis" is his key term: "The fiction movie exploits the possibilities of synthesis between photographic realism and dramatic illusion," he writes. "That synthesis, its value and implications, [is] the major subject of this study."

Unlike many latter-day theorists, who pay scant attention to the texts theory is supposed to illuminate, Perkins is a sharp critic who doesn't use theory to bully the reader or to deconstruct the films he chooses to discuss. Rather, his measured readings invite us to re-view specific films and to re-think our notions about the nature of film with a heightened awareness. Perkins is careful to temper the hero-worshipping tone that sometimes disfigures the work of critics inspired by the auteur theory, but he is nonetheles an auteurist at heart, and most of his insights spring from praise of directors he admires. That Hitchcock receives primary attention will not surprise contemporary readers, but Perkins' enthusiastic citations of Preminger, Richard Brooks, Vincente Minnelli, Samuel Fuller, Anthony Mann, and Nicholas Ray might. Like other early auteurists, Perkins enjoys ferreting significance from unexpected sources, uncovering art or at least subtlety in a system, the American commercial cinema, not then generally supposed to be capable of producing any. With a straight face he moves from close looks at canonical texts like *Psycho*, *Rope*, *The Birds*, and *Rear Window*, to detailed descriptions of exemplary scenes in unsung pictures like Minnelli's *The Courtship of Eddie's Father*, Preminger's *River of No Return*, *The Cardinal*, and *Exodus*, and Richard Brooks' *Elmer Gantry*, pointing out deft and integrated ways the directors have used lighting, decor, camera movement, costume, editing, and placement of actors. The kitchen scene in *The Courtship of Eddie's Father* commands as much space and respect as the shower scene in *Psycho*, but Perkins doesn't overload the obscure film with exaggerated claims. Here, as throughout, he assesses the value and depth of skillfully-made popular films with a critical level-headedness.

A humanist for whom the commercial narrative film that is his chosen beat is a form "in which thought and feeling are continually related to our common experience of the world," Perkins is distrustful of the film (and likewise the theory) that trades in code-cracking. "Films are not solely, or chiefly, valuable as crossword puzzles, in which the clues are difficult enough to make their solution gratifying, but not so difficult as to frustrate solution altogether." Perkins approaches films—movies—with the delight of the fan, and then submits the immediate raw experience of watching movies to an analysis that deepens the pleasure we seek in going to films in the first place. Without fuss, this stimulating book enlarges ways in which we can look at and listen to the screen. For civilians and specialists alike, *Film as Film* makes a lot of sense.

Foster Hirsch
New York
January 1993

Foster Hirsch is Professor of Film at Brooklyn College of the City University of New York and the author of numerous books on film and theatre, including Film Noir: The Dark Side of the Screen, A Method to Their Madness: The History of the Actors Studio, Laurence Olivier On Screen, Acting Hollywood Style, *and* Love, Sex, Death, and the Meaning of Life: The Films of Woody Allen. *He is now at work on a history of the Shuberts.*

Contents

Preface

This book aims to present criteria for our judgements of movies. It is written in the belief that film criticism becomes rational, if not 'objective', when it displays and inspects the nature of its evidence and the bases of its arguments.

The examples discussed are not drawn from the (rightly or wrongly) accepted classics of Film Art nor from the fashionable 'triumphs' of the past few years, but generally from films which seem to represent what the Movies meant to their public in the cinema's commercial heyday. I believe that the relevance and illustrative usefulness of these examples is to a large extent independent of the reader's memory or assessment of the particular films concerned. While the selection necessarily reflects areas of my own enthusiasm and knowledge, only some of my omissions are significant, and there is no correlation between my general estimate of the achievements of specific film-makers and the frequency or absence of references to their works.

The book would not have been started without stimulus and encouragement from my first editor at Penguin Books, the late Tony Richardson; its completion was greatly helped by the enthusiasm and understanding of Nikos Stangos. Many friends, colleagues and students have, knowingly or not, contributed to the development of the book's argument through discussion and debate. I particularly wish to acknowledge the contributions of those at the Berkshire College of Education, in the British Film Institute's Education Department, and on *Movie* magazine. I am more specifically indebted to Charles Barr and Sylvia Ellis who read draft manuscripts and offered useful suggestions and comments. Finally I can discover no aspect of the book's content and presentation which does not reflect the support and assistance given by my wife. For this reason, among others, it is very gratefully dedicated to her.

1 The Sins of the Pioneers

In 1911 William DeMille, who later became a prominent film-maker, described the movies as 'galloping tintypes [which] no one can expect . . . to develop into anything which could, by the wildest stretch of the imagination, be called art'.[1] Twenty-two years later the theorist Rudolph Arnheim noted: 'There are still many educated people who stoutly deny the possibility that film might be art. They say, in effect: "Film cannot be art, for it does nothing but reproduce reality mechanically." '[2] As late as 1947, the *Observer*'s film reviewer decided that films were nothing but 'bits of celluloid and wire', and thus felt 'ready to declare categorically that films are not an art. . . . It is not within the power of electrical engineering or mechanical contraption to create. They can only reproduce. And what they reproduce is not art.'

Statements like these were an important part of the background against which the theory of film was developed. Since the cinema was commonly despised by cultured persons, its partisans gave priority to boosting its status. Movie-going was to be vindicated as a respectable activity for men of intellect and refinement. One of the first theories of film in the English language was Vachel Lindsay's *The Art of the Moving Picture*. It was published in 1915 and described in its revised edition of 1922 as 'The Unchallenged Outline of Photoplay Critical Method'. The aim was openly propagandist. 'The motion picture art is a great high art,' Lindsay declared. 'The people I hope to convince of this are (1) the great art museums of America; (2) the departments of English, of the

1. Quoted by Lewis Jacobs, *The Rise of the American Film – A Critical History*, Harcourt, Brace, New York, 1956, p. 128.
2. Rudolph Arnheim, *Film as Art*, Faber & Faber, paperback edition, 1969, p. 17.

history of the drama, of the practice of the drama and the history and practice of art . . . (3) the critical and literary world generally.'[3]

This obsession with status persists in nearly all the standard works of film theory. D. W. Griffith's movie, *The Birth of a Nation*, made in 1914, is perhaps the earliest which critics could now agree to discuss without patronage or condescension. Paul Rotha's history *The Film Till Now* (1930) dismissed the film in a couple of paragraphs but added, 'if it achieved nothing else, it certainly placed the cinema as an entertainment and as a provocator of argument on the same level as the theatre and the novel. . . . The importance of the film lay in its achievement of attracting the notice of serious-minded people to the expressive power of the cinema.'[4] Twenty years after the appearance of Griffith's movie the serious-minded were still under siege; in 1933, Arnheim offered his study *Film* to 'the very people who might give the film its place among the arts . . . those who will accept a book but not a ticket for the "flicks", and those who still prefer the printed word to the moving picture'.[5]

We are more fortunately placed today. The battle for prestige has been won. The cultural establishments have been converted, though less by the evangelism of the theorists than by the good works of the film-makers. At the end of the fifties such pictures as Ingmar Bergman's *The Seventh Seal*, Alain Resnais's *Hiroshima Mon Amour* and Michelangelo Antonioni's *L'Avventura* offered carrion to the culture-vulture as rich and ripe as any provided by painting, music or literature. Of course, British universities have yet to recognize the significance of the cinema as an area of study. But even this failure seems the product of lethargy rather than scorn. With the achievements of the film-maker now celebrated in the press, analysed in specialist journals, and embalmed in archives throughout the world, we can do what Arnheim hoped to make possible for his readers: 'go to the pictures with a clearer conscience and fewer prejudices'.[6]

3. Vachel Lindsay, *The Art of the Moving Picture*, Liveright, New York, 1970, p. 45.
4. Paul Rotha, *The Film Till Now*, Vision Press, London, 1949, p. 151.
5. Rudolph Arnheim, *Film*, Faber & Faber, 1933, pp. 7–8.   6. ibid., p. 7.

Since victory has been secured and we enjoy its fruits, it might seem generous to forget the less dignified skirmishes, leave unquestioned the more dubious tactics and dwell only upon the fine enthusiasm and crusading zeal of the pioneers. Unfortunately, by putting film theory at the head of the attack they made it the campaign's chief casualty. It emerged radically deformed and incapable of useful growth. It could develop only as a sterile orthodoxy, a body of rules and prescriptions whose common features include internal contradiction and irrelevance to critical discussion of actual movies. The cinema which the great majority of film theorists present for our admiration is a fossil when it is not a myth. An aesthetic system established in the early years of the status struggle, and relevant to some aspects of the primitive form of cinema from which it was derived, has hardened into a dogma. It is re-stated with minor variants in all the standard texts of 'film appreciation', presenting what I shall call the *established* or *orthodox* theory of film.

The dogma not only fails to provide a coherent basis for discussion of particular films but actively obstructs understanding of the cinema. By examining both the theory itself and the pressures which gave rise to its distortions we should be able to clear the blockage and make way for more productive approaches.

The theorist's concern with prestige severely limited his freedom to investigate and speculate on the nature of the movies. His definitions had to be such that they would appeal to the conventionally cultured mind. Thus Lindsay 'endeavoured to keep to the established dogmas of Art' in the hope that 'the main lines of argument will appeal to the people who have classified and related the beautiful works of man that have preceded the moving pictures'.[7] The same hope was expressed by Arnheim when he set out to show that 'film art ... follows the same age-old canons and principles as every other art'.[8] These representative statements illustrate how the theorists appealed to first principles as the means of winning recognition for the cinema as the Seventh Art. They attempted to produce a definition of the medium of film which would coincide

7. Lindsay, op. cit., p. 215.
8. Arnheim, *Film*, p. 7.

with the definition of Art, by showing film to be subject to the same *age-old canons* and *established dogmas* as art in general.

This approach does more harm than good. It makes at least two unfounded assumptions. First, that we could derive the criteria appropriate to particular forms from a description of Art so broad as to include drama, music, novels, painting, poetry and sculpture; and second, that the theory of art is not itself problematic, having reached a level of clarity and coherence where it can both command general assent and serve the purpose of definition.

Supposing themselves to be dealing with definitions, film theorists submitted to fashionable prejudice. They did so at a time when received opinion was sure to be hostile to claims for the camera and its products. The years in which the movie evolved from a fascinating scientific curiosity into the major form of popular entertainment were also, not by coincidence, the years in which a decisive shift occurred in opinion about painting and the visual arts generally. Looking back from 1920 on the Post-Impressionist exhibition which he had presented nine years earlier, Roger Fry charted the shift. At the time of the exhibition 'the cultured public was determined to look upon Cézanne as an incompetent bungler and upon the whole movement as madly revolutionary. . . . Now that Matisse has become a safe investment for persons of taste. . . it will be difficult for people to imagine the vehemence of the indignation which greeted the first sight of [these] works in England.'[9] In 1912 Fry had explained this response as natural to 'a public which had come to admire above everything in a picture the skill with which the artist produced illusion. . . . The difficulty springs from a deep-rooted conviction due to long-established custom, that the aim of painting is the descriptive imitation of natural forms.'[10]

By the mid twenties the conviction had been so completely reversed that descriptive imitation was not only not required, it was highly suspect. The cultured public now inclined towards an attitude which Fry himself regarded as extreme. It is summarized in Clive Bell's view that 'if a representative form has value, it is as

9. Roger Fry, *Vision and Design*, Penguin, 1937, p. 228.
10. ibid., pp. 188–90.

form, not as representation. The representative element in a work of art may or may not be harmful; always it is irrelevant.'[11]

There was general acceptance also for Bell's opinion that the advent of photography had purified the painter's art, releasing it from an extraneous concern with description and representation, and thus redirecting its attention to essentials. By concentrating on the unique properties of their medium painters were recapturing the essence not just of things but of their own art.

The complexity of the relationship between camera, cinema and painting has been demonstrated elsewhere.[12] It is enough for us to note the irony of the following process: developments in painting, resulting largely from the impact of photography and film, promoted attitudes to art which film theory could accommodate only by performing gross contortions. The essence, the unique properties, of film had to be defined, but – given the fashionable divorce between creation and reproduction – defined in terms which denied or minimized the importance of the camera's function as a recorder of reality. The theorists committed themselves to overcoming what Lindsay described as 'the uncanny scientific quality of the camera's work'.[13]

This determination is seen at its most extreme in Rotha's lament that 'perhaps the greatest handicap imposed on aesthetic progress was the camera's misleading faculty of being able to record the actual'.[14] But a similar view underlies the whole of the established film theory. It is indeed one of the most important factors that unite, as creators or promoters of the orthodoxy, writers who display considerable variations of attitude and emphasis. All set out, with Bela Balazs in his *Theory of the Film*, to find the quality that the cinema 'does not *re*produce but produce and through which it becomes an independent, basically new art'.[15] All reach the same position as the Soviet film-maker and theorist Pudovkin: 'Between

11. Clive Bell, *Art*, Chatto & Windus, 1924, p. 25.
12. Aaron Scharf, *Art and Photography*, Allen Lane The Penguin Press, 1968.
13. Lindsay, op. cit., p. 222.
14. Rotha, op. cit., p. 88.
15. Bela Balazs, *Theory of the Film*, Dennis Dobson, 1952, p. 46.

the natural event and its appearance on the screen there is a marked difference. *It is exactly this difference* that makes the film an art.'[16] (My italics.)

Seen thus as the creative essence of the cinema, difference-from-reality is raised to the status of a criterion. Because 'art only begins where mechanical reproduction leaves off',[17] the orthodoxy puts a premium on the blatancy of the departure; the greater the difference the more manifest the Art. 'For anything to be a work of art,' Arnheim wrote, 'the medium employed must be obvious in the work itself. It is not enough to know that one is looking at a reproduction. The interplay of object and depictive medium must be patent in the finished work. The idiosyncrasies of the medium make themselves most felt in the greatest works of art.'[18]

When, in a similar vein, Lindsay predicted that the best film-makers would be 'those who emphasize the points wherein the photoplay is unique',[19] he clearly believed the *unique points* to be those derived from the properties of the projected celluloid strip. The foreword to his book described the artistic film as 'pattern in motion' and explained that 'pattern in this connection would imply an emphasis on the intrinsic suggestion of the spot and shape apart from their immediate relation to the appearance of natural objects'.[20]

This view of the cinema was most actively pursued in France. Before the First World War the French director Abel Gance described the cinema as the 'music of light'. A German colleague, Walter Ruttman, later affirmed that 'this music of light has always been and will remain the essence of cinema'.[21] In the late twenties Germaine Dulac, one of a group of French film-makers devoted to the concept of 'pure cinema', renewed Gance's analogy in her assertion that 'cinema and music have this in common: in both

16. V. I. Pudovkin, *Film Technique and Film Acting*, Vision: Mayflower Memorial Edition, London, 1958, p. 86.

17. Arnheim, *Film*, p. 69.

18. ibid., p. 45.

19. Lindsay, op. cit., p. 197.

20. ibid., p. xxiii.

21. Quoted by Henri Agel, *Esthétique du Cinéma*, Presses Universitaires de France, Paris, 1959, p. 24.

movement alone can create emotion by its rhythm and development'.[22] 'There is the symphony, pure music,' she wrote elsewhere. 'Why should the cinema not also have its symphony?'[23] The claim here is that the essence of a form can be found by isolating one of its components. Features other than essence will negate or dilute the form. But in music, for example, we never perceive 'movement alone'. It is always the movement of something which has its own characteristics, such as volume, pitch and timbre. The component described as essence cannot in practice be observed in a pure state.

Since they shared the isolating impulse, it was predictable that the purists' conception of cinema would appeal to orthodox theorists. Both Arnheim and Rotha proclaimed pure cinema the loftiest form of film art. The former 'would venture to predict that the film will be able to reach the heights of the other arts only when it frees itself from the bonds of photographic reproduction and becomes a pure work of man, namely, as animated cartoon or painting'.[24] Rotha, defining the cinema as 'light revealed by moving form', amused himself by building a hierarchy of forms in which 'the abstraction of the "absolute" film is the nearest approach to the purest form of cinema. . . . Following this, there will be determined the other forms of cinema, descending in aesthetic significance through the epic and art film to the ordinary narrative film and the singing and dancing picture.'[25]

However violently we reject Rotha's hierarchy of forms, the least that can be said for his position, and Arnheim's, is that the commitment to purism represents a logical extension of tendencies built into established theory by the effort to annex film to the recognized media. In the conditions of the silent era, such an attempt necessarily led towards a model derived from the visual arts; 'pattern in motion' offered the most persuasive evidence that the cinema could create a unique extension of existing forms whilst

22. ibid., p. 12.
23. Quoted in Siegfried Kracauer, *Theory of Film*, Galaxy, Oxford University Press, New York, 1965, p. 183.
24. Arnheim, *Film as Art*, p. 175.
25. Rotha, op. cit., p. 88.

depending neither on the reproduction of reality nor on an *inferior* duplication of other media.

The threat to the cinema's status, if it did not follow this route, was indicated by Balazs: 'Everything had first to be reality before it could become a picture. Hence the film we see on the screen is merely a photographic reproduction, or, to be exact, the reproduction of a histrionic performance.'[26] The danger was that if the movie were not shown to be an extension of visual art, it would be seen as a corruption of drama. It would be exposed as 'canned theatre', drama without the power of speech and thus deprived of its most powerful resource. The cinema would rightly be despised as a mere dumb-show. The theatre critic George Jean Nathan laid the charge in 1928:

> The movie as we see it by and large at the present time is simply a stage play, its unities corrupted, stripped of its words, and made to show all the scenes and episodes that the dramatist has, with artistic economy, laboriously succeeded either in deleting from his work or in keeping off the stage.[27]

In order to repudiate calumnies of this sort the orthodox theorists joined Arnheim in rejecting 'effects that are also possible on the stage'.[28] 'Theatrical' became, and has remained, the most contemptuous adjective in the theorist's vocabulary, being used to indicate that the filming has *added* nothing to the recorded event.

But the purist view did not enter the mainstream of established theory. Rotha and Arnheim themselves proclaimed supremacy of the abstract movie in a marginal, even nostalgic way. The theorists refused the logic of the 'visual art' position. Working from the same preconceptions, they tried nevertheless to accommodate the fact that what was seen on the screen had been derived, in most cases, from a pre-existing reality. Their model, fine art, imposed the view that the real scene or human figure had no artistic relevance; what mattered was the way it was *rendered* in paint and marble, or on film. The resulting dislocations can be seen in the

26. Balazs, op. cit., p. 46.
27. George Jean Nathan, *Art of the Night*, Alfred A. Knopf, London, 1928, p. 117.
28. Arnheim, *Film as Art*, p. 131.

theorists' inability to find the recorded action a place in the critical scheme or to allow it any artistic status. The object in front of the camera was simply reality. The important concern was with the way in which the act or process of cinematography could be shown to impose a pattern on that reality.

When Arnheim declares a particular film episode to be 'cine-matographic inasmuch as a definite feature of film technique is being used as a means to secure an effect',[29] it is clear that he sees film technique overwhelmingly in terms of the peculiarities of camera, lenses, and film stocks. The manner of recording, here and throughout established theory, is given a quite artificial precedence over what is recorded. It is as if a theory of poetry were to acknow-ledge that words refer to things but insist that the critical reader should be concerned with their sounds alone. The orthodoxy defines the medium as 'film', meaning the stuff that goes through the camera, whereas the subject of criticism is actually the movie, the thing we see on the screen.

Given this false definition of the medium, the theorists' concern with its unique properties was inevitably misleading. Film theory became established as the embodiment of twin mystiques, one of the *image* and the other of *montage*.

The mystique of the image was partially developed before the cinema's arrival. Still photographers had long been urged to produce work which could be judged by the same criteria as painting. Newhall's *History of Photography* reports the suggestion made by Sir William Newton in 1853 that photographers ought to alter their pictures so as to conform to the 'acknowledged prin-ciples of Fine Art'.[30] Following a similar argument Lindsay created chapter headings such as 'Sculpture in Motion', and asked his readers to 'consider: first came the photograph. Then motion was added to the photograph. We must use this order in our judge-ment. If it is ever to evolve into a national art, it must first be good picture, then good motion.'[31] The people best qualified to produce

29. ibid., p. 39.
30. Beaumont Newhall, *The History of Photography from 1839 to the Present Day*, Museum of Modern Art, New York, 1949, pp. 17-18.
31. Lindsay, op. cit., p. 135.

'the higher photoplays', Lindsay concluded, were painters, sculptors and architects. Lindsay's emphasis on the decorative qualities of the film image is very much a reflection of his time. It is a remnant of the period in which 'all speculations on aesthetic had revolved with wearisome persistence around the question of the nature of beauty. . . . We sought for the criteria of the beautiful, whether in art or nature.'[32] Pictorial criteria were absorbed into the orthodoxy. They were stressed in one of its later statements, Roger Manvell's *Film*: 'Composition is all-important: everything photographed becomes a two-dimensional pattern.'[33] This derives from Arnheim's treatment of the 'Artistic Utilization of Reduced Depth': 'Every good film shot is satisfying in a purely formal sense as a linear composition. The lines are harmoniously disposed with reference to one another as well as to the margins. The distribution of light and shade in the shot is evenly balanced.'[34]

But Arnheim gives less weight to decorative requirements than to demands for a meaningfully organized image. Theorists after Lindsay continued to expect the camera to create beauty but responded to developments in painting, criticism and film-making (whose influence Lindsay had escaped) by demanding much more emphatically that it create significance. In a chapter revealingly titled 'The Creative Camera', Balazs writes that camera angle is 'the strongest means of characterization the film possesses; and it is not reproduction but genuine production.'[35] The mystique of the image insists that the attributes of the camera be employed expressively. It favours the overt use of photographic devices of selection and distortion as a means of commenting upon objects and events. Uses of the camera which seem to depend primarily on its reliability as a recording instrument, or on the realistic appearance of its products, are dismissed as uncinematic, a neglect of the medium.

Thus, although he admired Chaplin enormously, Arnheim felt obliged to concede that his pictures were 'not really "filmic"

32. Fry, op. cit., p. 229.
33. Roger Manvell, *Film*, Penguin Books, 1950, p. 28.
34. Arnheim, *Film as Art*, p. 56.
35. Balazs, op. cit., p. 46.

(because his camera serves mainly as a recording machine)'.[36] And Rotha was so impressed by the determinedly bizarre décor of Robert Weine's expressionist picture *The Cabinet of Dr Caligari* ('The first real aesthetic advance in the cinema ... the first genuinely imaginative film ... the first attempt at the expression of a creative mind in the new medium ...')[37] that he lost all taste for settings that looked authentic. He lists as one of the 'chief faults' of *The Birth of a Nation* 'the realistic replicas of Abraham Lincoln's study and the theatre in which he was assassinated'.[38]

The mystique of the image grows out of the classification of film as a visual art. The point at issue is not the ability of the film image to meet certain criteria derived from painting; empirically that point has been settled by a host of directors. But the 'visual art' category created confusion when it was seen to imply the universal validity of criteria which are applicable only to limited, artistically optional, aspects of film-making. As a result, the decorative and expressive use of pictorial space was given precedence over the dramatic use of real space. Established theory commands the camera to *create* and denies its right to observe. The mystique of the image entered into the orthodoxy as soon as the facilities of the camera were converted into the 'demands of the medium'.

All the visual resources of the cinema were not, however, thought sufficient to refute the charge that film-making was a mechanical process. The action recorded by the camera might be modified by composition, lighting and the whole apparatus of the 'pattern in motion', but it was recorded action nonetheless.

Conclusive evidence was still needed that the process of film-making allowed as great a control over reality as any other medium. Orthodox theory found this in the mystique of montage. Hence Balazs: 'Montage, the mobile architecture of the film's picture material, is a specific, new creative art.'[39] Although it has acquired special 'creative' connotations, 'montage' is just the French word for film editing. Since celluloid strips can be cut and joined at any

36. Arnheim, *Film as Art*, p. 93.
37. Rotha, op. cit., p. 93.
38. ibid., p. 151.
39. Balazs, op. cit., p. 46.

point, a film-maker can assume complete control over those elements of time and space which are reproduced more or less automatically in the images. He can unite events which are far apart or dissect those which are continuous. During the movie's silent period the implications of this fact were explored, intuitively in the United States by Edwin S. Porter and D. W. Griffith, more systematically in the Soviet Union by many directors – most notably S. M. Eisenstein and V. I. Pudovkin, both of whom wrote extremely influential works on film aesthetics. By building his picture from a sequence of details the film-maker extended his ability to highlight the significant aspects of the action and to control the rhythm of the movie.

Most important, because it most conclusively demonstrated the 'creative' nature of editing, was the discovery that when two shots were joined together the spectator might be made to infer a variety of contrasts and comparisons between two sets of information. In *The End of St Petersburg* (1927) Pudovkin cut back and forth between shots of Russian soldiers dying on the battlefield and shots of the stock exchange blackboard as share prices soared. 'It is impossible for the spectator not to see a causal connection,' said Balazs.[40] However, the spectator's conclusion – 'Capitalists thrive on war and profit from the miseries of the common man' – would not have been suggested by either set of shots on its own. Pudovkin *created* the concept in his montage by interrelating two distinct phenomena. 'The single shots,' Balazs wrote, 'are saturated with the tension of a latent meaning which is released like an electric spark when the next shot is joined to it.'[41] Eisenstein went even further: 'Two film pieces of any kind, placed together, inevitably combine into a new concept, a new quality, arising out of that juxtaposition.'[42] And, a little further in the same essay:

The juxtaposition of two separate shots by splicing them together resembles not so much a simple sum of one shot plus another shot – as

40. ibid., p. 128.
41. ibid., p. 118.
42. Sergei Eisenstein, *Film Form* and *The Film Sense*, Meridian Books, New York. 1957: *The Film Sense*, p. 4.

it does a *creation*. It resembles a creation – rather than the sum of its parts – from the circumstance that in every such juxtaposition *the result is qualitatively* distinguishable from each component element viewed separately.[43]

The idea that editing 'resembles a creation' dominated the development of the orthodoxy. Editing became identified with the creative *language* of the cinema. In his book *Film Technique* Pudovkin stated that 'to the film director each shot of the finished film subserves the same purpose as the word to the poet';[44] and later: 'Editing is the language of the film director. Just as in living speech, so, one may say, in editing: there is a word – the piece of exposed film, the image; a phrase – the combination of these pieces.'[45]

Even if we accept Pudovkin's view of language (and even when we relate it to very special cases like the sequence quoted from his own picture), the parallel between images and words is greatly exaggerated. The simplest close-up in the crudest silent film shows much more than can be expressed in one word. Language separates the different aspects of a single phenomenon by its use of nouns, verbs, adjectives and so on; but on film, even edited film, the object (noun) cannot be dissociated from what it does (verb) or how it looks (adjective). The more complex the content of a shot, the less relevant the verbal parallels become. That is one reason why established theory requires the recorded event to be broken down into relatively simple units. If an action is filmed as a selection of details, the montage becomes an active and obvious source of 'meaning' in the assembled sequence. Hence Balazs places great value on close-ups as 'the pictures expressing the poetic sensibility of the director'.[46] If editing could be considered as the uniquely *creative* stage in film-making it would be reasonable to say, with Pudovkin, that 'only by his editing methods can one judge a director's individuality';[47] with the historian Lewis Jacobs that 'the intensity

43. ibid., pp. 7–8.
44. Pudovkin, op. cit., p. 24.
45. ibid., p. 100.
46. Balazs, op. cit., p. 56.
47. Pudovkin, op. cit., p. 100.

and subtlety of a director's editing are the indices of his craftsmanship';[48] or with Balazs, that 'it is in [montage] that the individual
creativeness of a film-maker chiefly manifests itself'.[49]

The ultimate and least valid extension of the mystique is the
belief that montage provides not just the *language* of film, but a
definition of the movie's artistic nature: in Rotha's words 'the
intrinsic essence of filmic creation'.[50] This idea was originally
propounded by the Soviet theorists. Pudovkin absorbed and
reported the views of the researcher and teacher, Lev Kuleshov:

All he said was this: 'In every art there must be first a material, and
secondly, a method of composing this material specially adapted to
this art' ... Kuleshov maintained that the material in film-work
consists of pieces of film, and that the composition method is their
joining together in a particular, creatively discovered order. He maintained that the film-art does not begin when the artists act and the
various scenes are shot – this is only the preparation of the material.
Film-art begins from the moment when the director begins to combine
and join the various pieces of film.[51]

On his own behalf Pudovkin advanced the claim

that every object, taken from a given viewpoint and shown on the
screen to spectators, is a *dead object*, even though it has moved before
the camera ... Only if the object be placed together among a number
of separate objects, only if it be presented as part of a synthesis of
different separate visual images, is it endowed with filmic life.[52]

The emphasis on one aspect of film-making at the expense of all
others has two main results. It unbalances our view of the movies
by concentrating attention on the one process which is held to be
creative. But it diminishes our understanding of that process too.
An artificial distinction between 'material' and 'organization'
obscures the real importance of editing since it limits rather than
extends the film-maker's powers of selection. While it encourages

48. Lewis Jacobs, op. cit., p. 50.
49. Balazs, op. cit., p. 31.
50. Rotha, op. cit., p. 93.
51. Pudovkin, op. cit., pp. 166–7.
52. ibid., p. 25.

him to choose freely the details which he wishes to isolate in order to construct his pattern, it demands that he construct the pattern from isolated details. It requires him to organize in a specific, arbitrarily favoured way, and thus converts a technical resource into an artistic obligation. For example, by tying the concept of rhythm to the duration of the shots it produces a crude formula which offers no approach to the rhythmic subtleties of films like Jean Renoir's *La Règle du Jeu* and Max Ophuls's *Letter from an Unknown Woman*. These pictures employ a rhythmic counterpoint which editing assists but which it certainly does not create.

If we isolate cutting from the complex which includes the movements of the actors, the shape of the setting, the movement of the camera, and variations of light and shade – which change *within* the separate shots as well as between them – we shall understand none of the elements (and certainly not the editing) because each of them derives its value from its relationship with the others. The least to be said here is that Ophuls and Renoir are not such obviously negligible artists that film theory can afford to leave their work out of account. But the orthodoxy has to exclude them. It can accommodate only films which allow a clear distinction between 'material' and 'composition'. Such a distinction results from and depends on identifying the material as 'mere reality'. Ernest Lindgren's compendium of established theory, *The Art of the Film*, shows this in its discussion and endorsement of editing as the 'foundation of film art':

> Only if the film itself can be utilized to mould and shape the event, to express an attitude towards it, to express something of the impact it makes on the artist as an experience, has it any claim to be an art form. It is true . . . that by the choice of a particular viewpoint for the camera a certain overtone of significance can be implied within the limits of a single shot or even frame, but the potentialities of this device are extremely limited. On the other hand, as soon as we resort to editing . . . [53]

The 'limits of the single shot' are those imposed by the theorist. Its potentialities are restricted by the insistence upon brief fragments of detail. The orthodox theorist is unwilling to examine the

53. Ernest Lindgren, *The Art of the Film*, Allen & Unwin, 1963, p. 79.

complexity of organization which film-makers like Hitchcock, Keaton, Murnau, and Welles have achieved within the sustained shot. He demands that the 'event' be dissected in the shooting and reconstituted in the montage because he refuses to allow the event itself any significance; it can be moulded and shaped only by the techniques of cinematography. It has an *impact* on the artist which he expresses in his manner of shooting and cutting. Lindgren's account thus ignores the possibility that the artist may create rather than just respond 'artistically' to events, that the recorded action may itself have been shaped and moulded so as to become significant. His argument betrays the basic inadequacy of established theory: 'action' is equated with 'mere reality', since it is treated as if it existed outside the area of control. A similar attitude applied to writing would equate the novel with journalism. The orthodox theorists have been unable to formulate criteria which take account of the difference between reality and fiction. Systematically emphasizing the cinema's properties as a visual medium, their theory neglects or denigrates the aspects which the movie shares with narrative forms, especially dramatic ones. Because it is unable to locate what happens on the screen *within* the medium of film, the orthodoxy presents narrative as an alien form which the movie may translate and annotate but not absorb as part of its creative mechanism.

The reasoning is false. Story-telling, the representation of imagined action, is not an autonomous form but one which both assumes and informs the character of the medium used in the telling. It is not opposed to poetry, novel, strip-cartoon or theatre, and it cannot reasonably be seen as hostile or irrelevant to cinema. The movie incorporates the real object or fictional event into the medium itself. The basic vocabulary of photography recognizes this; 'raw' film is 'exposed' to the features of the given subject but 'developed' only when it reveals the image derived from them. The camera *is* primarily a recording instrument. It does not always *add* significantly to what it records, but its ability to select, mould, heighten, or comment upon events is a consequence of its ability to record them. That allows the film-maker to stage for the camera rather as the composer writes for the instrument. He can shape the action in terms of its destiny – reproduction on the cinema screen.

Once the created event is recognized, films begin to acquire many of the characteristics of novels and plays. What is presented becomes a part of the manner of presentation. Events, personalities and motives are subject to control alongside pattern, movement and rhythm. When he works with actors the film director assumes many of the functions of his theatrical counterpart. He organizes the space in front of the camera much as the stage director controls the space beyond the proscenium. Gesture, grouping, pace, intonation and movement can become vitally significant. But according to Lindgren a film-maker either expresses himself through editing or 'he will fall back on glib, superficial and essentially non-filmic methods such as relying on his actors and using cinematography simply to record their performance'.[54] Lewis Jacobs provides the *reductio ad absurdum* of the theory. He first claims that 'in movie-making, guiding the camera, even more than directing the actor, is the trick',[55] but later describes the camera itself as 'an essential but nevertheless subordinate tool to the cutting process'.[56] With actors and action relegated to the same base level as mere reality, the theory can offer nothing more than a technical dogma in which the demands of the medium are upheld at the expense of its possibilities. While it claims to provide artistic criteria for the spectator, it imposes rules on the film-maker. Thus Lindgren's 'criteria' are aptly expressed in the form of an interrogation: 'Is this film filmic? By which I mean: Does it use the language of the motion picture?... Does it build up its total effect by a composition of visual details, skilfully selected and welded together by means of editing?'[57]

A false definition of film makes the demand for the filmic a critical catastrophe. It leaves us without standards to distinguish between even those movies which follow 'correct' methods. Incapable of giving adequate weight to the complexities of the

54. ibid., p. 167.
55. Lewis Jacobs, op. cit., p. 110.
56. ibid., p. 313.
57. Lindgren, op. cit., p. 166.

medium, established theory finds artistic excellence in expressive devices rather than significant style. As a result, it tends always to value rhetoric and bombast at the expense of subtlety. Orthodox writings characteristically present crude and laborious 'effects' as models of filmic creation. The preferred movies are most often works of propaganda in which subtlety or complexity would contradict the *raison d'être*. The theory offers no standards by which we could define the stylistic grossness of such a film as Leni Riefenstahl's *Triumph of the Will*, a record of the Nüremberg Rally of 1936, which set out to glorify Nazi ambitions and personalities. The picture's effect, such as it is and however contemptible, was certainly built up by strict adherence to the Lindgren formula. At the other end of the scale, the orthodoxy's prescriptions exclude many works which a theory of film should at least enable us to discuss, and many also which the theorists themselves claim to admire. Lindgren, for instance, finds in the movies of Buñuel and Bergman, among others, 'personal expression of a quality not realized by any of their predecessors'.[58] Yet each of them regularly falls back on the methods which Lindgren condemns as non-filmic. We may with Lindgren also regard Von Stroheim's *Greed* as a masterpiece; but the film cannot be made to fit the theorist's criteria. Few movies have made *less* use of edited details. If ever a director favoured accumulation over selection, it was the maker of *Greed*. According to the dogma *Greed* does not exist, since 'if a cinematograph production is not filmic there is no film in the proper sense to criticize'.[59]

This gulf between theoretical criteria and proclaimed enthusiasms shows how little the orthodox view of the cinema owes and contributes to a consideration of actual movies. It treats artistry in terms of methods rather than of works, as if a 'correct' use of the medium would itself provide both a guarantee and a standard of excellence.

As a result, the theory is most emphatic where it should be most cautious, in imposing obligations on the artist; it is least helpful where it should be most relevant, in developing the disciplines of

58. ibid., p. 207.
59. ibid., p. 167.

criticism. A useful theory will have to redirect attention to the movie as it is *seen*, by shifting the emphasis back from creation to perception. In order to arrive at a more accurate and inclusive definition of film as it exists for the spectator, it will need to concentrate not on the viewfinder and the cutting bench but on the screen.

2 Minority Reports

One of the things which the spectator finds on the screen is a photograph. The defects of orthodox theory spring from its inability to handle the implications of this crucial fact. But other writers have tried to place the 'uncanny scientific quality' of the camera's products within a theoretical framework rather than on its margins. The French critic André Bazin was the most important of these.

In a series of articles published between 1944 and his death in 1958, Bazin argued that a film aesthetic must, at least, take account of the nature and function of photography. He never wrote a 'theory of film' as such; his chief work, four volumes titled *What Is the Cinema?*, is simply a selection from his most important articles. As a practising critic, Bazin was less inclined than most theorists to separate abstract speculation on the cinema from day-to-day experience of the movies.

For Bazin the cinema was essentially 'the art of reality'. In the preface to his collected work, he described his line of thought:

We shall begin, necessarily, with the photographic image, the primitive element of the ultimate synthesis, and go on from there to outline, if not a theory of film language based on the hypothesis of its inherent realism, at least an analysis which in no way contradicts it.[1]

The invention of photography, he argued, finally satisfied the demand (which other visual arts had long attempted to meet) for a magical process which could order and possess the natural world by capturing its image, and resist the ravages of time by 'fixing' the image of a single moment. Photography satisfied this

1. André Bazin, *Qu'est-ce que le Cinéma?*, 4 vols., Les Éditions du Cerf, Paris, 1958, 1959, 1961, 1962. Vol. I, p. 9.

need more conclusively than, for example, painting, because its mechanical nature made it absorb the features of the visible world without interpretation: the personality of the artist did not intervene between the world and its image. 'All the arts depend on the presence of man; only photography lets us delight in his absence.'[2] The cinema, which extended the power of the camera through time, derived its nature from that of photography and its aesthetic appeal came from the same source; the revelation of reality.

Bazin was not the only, or even the first, writer to put forward this view (though he stated it more systematically and with a greater awareness of its implications than anyone else). In the early twenties Marcel L'Herbier had already described the cinema as 'l'art du réel' and claimed that its vocation was to 'transcribe with as much fidelity and accuracy as possible, without transposition or stylization, and by the methods of exactitude which are specific to it, a certain phenomenal truth'.[3]

Siegfried Kracauer's book *Theory of Film: The Redemption o, Physical Reality*, first published in 1960, adopted Bazin's premises but applied them with less coherence and a more obscure, at times impenetrable, line of reasoning. His basic position, however, was clear enough:

Film is essentially an extension of photography and therefore shares with this medium a marked affinity for the visible world around us. Films come into their own when they record and reveal physical reality ... [and] are true to the medium to the extent that they penetrate the world before our eyes.[4]

The objectivity of the photographic image was thus seen to distinguish the movies from other forms: a sonnet or a sonata created *a* world which might reflect the subjective vision of its maker; film recorded *the* world which existed objectively. The 'art of reality' was therefore an art with a very great difference. Bazin

2. ibid., p. 15.
3. Quoted by Agel, *Esthétique du Cinéma*, p. 40.
4. Kracauer, *Theory of Film*, Oxford University Press, New York, 1965, p. ix.

delighted in analysing films which were aesthetically satisfying primarily because their makers had renounced the privileges of the creator for the duties of the explorer or investigator. The 'inexhaustible paradox' of film used as a scientific instrument was that 'when research is most completely self-centred and functional, and absolutely devoid of any aesthetic intention, cinematographic beauty is brought into being as an unexpected bonus'.[5] In another essay he claimed that 'chance and reality have more talent than all the world's film-makers'.[6]

Kracauer too insisted that the attempt to secure the cinema's recognition as Art confused, rather than clarified, the important issues. The use of the word 'art' in relation to movies 'tends to obscure the aesthetic value of films which are really true to the medium'[7] because 'the intrusion of Art into film thwarts the cinema's intrinsic possibilities. If for reasons of aesthetic purity films influenced by the traditional arts prefer to disregard actual physical reality, they miss an opportunity reserved for the cinematic medium.'[8]

But if the cinema is most true to itself when it absorbs reality, what claim can it have to our attention? Does the image of an event differ sufficiently from the event itself to make it worth our while to watch in the cinema things which we could observe in the world at large?

To this problem Bazin and Kracauer propose essentially the same solution: reality differs from its photographic image to the extent that our way of seeing reality differs from our way of seeing films. The cinema breaks through the barrier of convention, ideology and prejudice which constricts our view of reality. According to Kracauer:

In recording and exploring physical reality, film exposes to view a world never seen before ... physical nature has been persistently veiled by ideologies relating its manifestations to some total aspect of the universe ... The truly decisive reason for the elusiveness of physical

5. Bazin, op. cit., Vol. I, p. 37.
6. ibid., p. 43.
7. Kracauer, op. cit., p. 39.
8. ibid., p. 301.

reality is the habit of abstract thinking we have acquired under the reign of science and technology.[9]

In Bazin's view,

Only the impartiality of the lens can clear the object of habit and prejudice, of all the mental fog with which our perception blurs it, and present it afresh for our attention and thereby for our affection. In a photograph, the natural image of a world we don't know how to see, nature finally imitates not just art, but the artist himself.[10]

In the Bazin-Kracauer view respect for reality becomes a criterion. Bazin's work reflects the development of the cinema during the time that he practised criticism; his theory was directly linked to the most distinctive movement of the post-war years. Italian 'neo-realism', represented by the films of, for example, de Sica (*Bicycle Thieves, Umberto D*), Fellini (*I Vitelloni, The Nights of Cabiria*), and Rossellini (*Paisa, Open City*), seemed 'an exemplary tendency in today's cinema'. In his analysis of Fellini's *La Strada*, Bazin described his ideal: 'I would not say that the camera flatly photographs [the object], even the word photography would be an exaggeration, it quite simply shows the object, or better still, allows us to see it.'[11]

By submitting to reality, the film-maker in no way relinquished his creative role: the facts about men and society were as difficult to communicate as any subjective vision.

There has never been a form of 'realism' in art which was not first of all profoundly 'aesthetic' . . . In art, reality, like imagination, belongs only to the artist, the flesh and blood of reality are no easier to embody in the textures of literature or cinema than imagination's most gratuitous fantasies.[12]

Reality was greater than any one view of it, and the film-maker's first duty was to the objects and events depicted, not to his beliefs about them. Bazin admired the neo-realist cinema for 'the priority

9. ibid., pp. 299–300.
10. Bazin, op. cit., Vol. I, p. 18.
11. Bazin, op. cit., Vol. IV, p. 124.
12. ibid., p. 20.

given to the representation of reality over dramatic structures'.[13]
The Italian directors all criticized society,

> but they have learned, even while stating their attitudes most clearly,
> never to treat reality as a means. To condemn it does not demand
> falsification. They remember that, before it is contemptible, the world,
> quite simply, *exists* . . . Facts are facts; our imagination makes use of
> them, but they are not designed *a priori* to serve it.[14]

The 'realist' view of the cinema evidently called in question the
whole of the orthodox theory. In particular, editing – far from
being the essential source of 'film art' – became extremely suspect
because it sacrificed the natural relationship between an object and
its context in order to construct an arbitrary relationship between
shots. Bazin thought the 'dictum that the cinema began as an art
with montage has been temporarily productive but its virtues are
exhausted'.[15]

Montage on the Russian pattern was designed to demonstrate
an attitude rather than to show an event; as a result it constantly
isolated objects and actions from the background which made
them significant, and forced them to take on a significance of the
director's own creation. Bazin offered this definition of montage
which, though hostile, was very close to one of Eisenstein's: 'the
creation of a meaning which the images do not objectively contain
and which proceeds only from their relationship'.[16]

Editing further depreciated the reality portrayed, by imposing a
single meaning on any one phenomenon. Kracauer somehow
managed to reconcile a belief in film as a revelation of physical
reality with the assertion that 'of all the technical properties of film
the most general and indispensable is editing'.[17] However, he
rejoined Bazin in maintaining that reality is ambiguous and that
films should respect that ambiguity:

> Natural objects are surrounded with a fringe of meanings liable to

13. ibid., p. 138.
14. ibid., p. 15.
15. Bazin, op. cit., Vol. I, p. 74.
16. ibid., p. 133.
17. Kracauer, op. cit., p. 29.

touch off various moods, emotions, runs of inarticulate thoughts ... A film shot does not come into its own unless it incorporates raw material with its multiple meanings or what Lucien Sève calls 'the anonymous state of reality'.[18]

But the montage of the Russian school suppressed the 'multiple meanings' in order to impose a single view of an amorphous reality. The spectator was required to take on trust the significance attached to an event (as in the anti-capitalist montage in *The End of St Petersburg*) and was prevented from finding any other meaning in it than the one dictated by the cutting. Montage, said Bazin, 'is essentially and by its very nature opposed to the expression of ambiguity'.[19]

At the same time, it favoured the lazy or the stupid spectator, and encouraged him in his defects. Constantly drawing attention to its own significance, the montage film presupposed the docility of the viewer and relieved him of the responsibility of making connections between, and drawing conclusions from, the events presented. He would gain nothing by scrutinizing the image since the montage sequence would make sense only in the terms dictated by the director. Here again Bazin was representing in an unfavourable light a view propounded by Eisenstein:

> The strength of montage resides in this, that it includes in the creative process the emotions and mind of the spectator. The spectator is compelled to proceed along that selfsame creative road that the author travelled in creating the image.[20]

In devaluing 'expressive' montage Bazin was attempting to bring film theory into line with current practice. Directors like Jean Renoir, Orson Welles, and William Wyler had to a large extent renounced editing effects in order to explore the dramatic possibilities of an uninterrupted continuity in space and time. Bazin drew gleeful attention to the wide range of events which depended on the spatial relationship between man and object; to break these events down according to the customary 'cinematic' formula of

18. ibid., pp. 68–9.
19. Bazin, op. cit., Vol. I, p. 144.
20. Eisenstein, *The Film Sense*, p. 32.

edited close-ups would have been to destroy their meaning and effect.

In Robert Flaherty's documentary of Eskimo life, *Nanook of the North* (1920), there was a sequence which showed Nanook fishing for seal through a hole in the Arctic ice; the bait was taken and, after a long struggle, Nanook managed to heave the seal out on to the ice and capture it. The whole episode was filmed from one position which showed both Nanook and the hole, the emergence of the seal, and finally the struggle between hunter and hunted. Bazin pointed out that it could not, effectively, be presented otherwise. If Flaherty had cut back and forth between close-ups of Nanook and the hole, Nanook and the seal, the impact of the sequence would have been lost. The contest existed in space. Since the distance between Nanook and the seal was the source of the drama, the episode could not have been presented effectively by a technique which disrupted its continuity in space. The suspense of the struggle would have been dissipated if we had not been able to follow exactly from one moment to the next the varying fortunes of Nanook and his intended victim. In circumstances like these, Bazin said,

montage, which they so often tell us is the essence of the cinema, is the literary and anti-cinematic process par excellence: the unique quality of film, captured for once in its pure state, depends upon a simple photographic respect for the unity of space.[21]

Bazin's view admitted into the ranks of legitimate cinema much that the orthodox theorist was obliged to condemn. In particular, great clowns like Keaton and Chaplin could now be discussed as film-makers rather than as vaudeville artists whose acts happened to have been recorded on film. In Buster Keaton's *The Navigator* there arrived, through a splendid combination of oversight and misfortune, a moment when Buster's leg was tangled with a string which in turn connected to a miniature cannon, loaded and ready to function. Every time Buster tried to move out of its line of fire his leg jerked the string and pulled the cannon round on target again. No amount of cutting between Buster and the cannon,

21. Bazin, op. cit., Vol. I, p. 123.

however menacingly presented, could have improved the treacherous precision with which the weapon traced the movements of the hero's leg.

Keaton's camera was quite uncreative. It reported the incident as impassively as Keaton portrayed it, changing position not for effect but simply in order to maintain the spectator's view of some highly mobile proceedings. Where the orthodoxy would have to present this as mere recording, Bazin's theory would accommodate it as one of the 'situations which exist cinematographically only to the extent that their spatial unity is displayed, [the most notable example being] comic situations based on relationships between men and objects'.[22]

Even in sequences which are not, strictly, dependent upon an exact time-space relationship, there are often advantages to be derived from procedures which limit the camera's freedom to select and interpret. Louis Feuillade, an early French master, included an episode in one of his serials, *Tih Minh* (1918), in which the heroine, Tih herself, hid in a picnic basket in order to accompany her guardian on one of his adventures. The basket was placed on top of his car and the journey began. As the car emerged from a tunnel at the bottom of a cliff, one of the villains secured the basket with a rope and the others pulled it up to the top of the cliff. The camera watched the villains as they heaved the basket up, but we could still see the car – very small in the background of the picture – as it continued on its way along the coast road. Throughout the time that the villains were unlocking the basket and binding Tih Minh we were able to watch the car as it followed the road twisting away in the distance. It sailed on round a bend and out of sight, reappeared farther away, and finally disappeared from sight when the road turned round the cliff on our horizon.

The least one can say for Feuillade's treatment of this long episode is that it was as effective as any editing arrangement in conveying the hero's total unawareness that anything was amiss and in making us feel the gradual draining of hope for the heroine's rescue. But I think one can go further than this. Any shot which interrupted the continuity of the sequence in order to *show* us the

22. ibid., p. 129.

unperturbed hero would have reduced its suspense. Because we could only watch the car's journey and infer the hero's ignorance from its progress, we were able to maintain a hope that it would stop, or turn round and retrace its tracks (there were complicated reasons why it might have done so). And in fact the first time the car went out of sight we were able to imagine that, when it next appeared, it might be coming back towards us. When it *did* reappear, even farther away, our disappointment was all the greater; the particular effect of this sequence would have been destroyed by an editing pattern which let us know what was happening in the car. A different drama might have been created. But there are no grounds for supposing that it would have been superior in substance or effect to the one offered by Feuillade.

Tih Minh, Nanook of the North, and *The Navigator* were all made and shown before the established theory became established, but it offers no place for their methods. Bazin accused the orthodox theorists of 'mistaking the alleged primacy of the image for the true vocation of the cinema which is the primacy of the object'.[23] He drew a distinction between two lines of development in the silent cinema. The one, followed primarily by the Russian school, was based on the image, 'everything which the method of representation on the screen could add to the thing represented'.[24]

For this group the silent cinema was virtually a complete instrument; 'at the very most sound would be able to play only a subordinate and complementary role: as a counterpoint to the image'.[25] The second took reality as its basis: 'here the image counts in the first place not for what it *adds* to reality, but for what it *reveals* of reality'.[26]

The films of Stroheim, Murnau, Flaherty, and Carl Dreyer, Bazin thought,

represented the most productive vein of the so-called silent cinema, the only one which, just because the essence of its aesthetic was not bound up with montage, required the realism of sound as a natural extension

23. Bazin, op. cit., Vol. II, p. 48.
24. Bazin, op. cit., Vol. I, p. 132.
25. ibid., p. 134.
26. ibid., p. 135.

... It is true that the talkie rang the death knell for a particular aesthetic of the cinematographic language, but only for the one which carried it furthest away from its realist vocation.[27]

In these remarks Bazin echoed the content of orthodox theory while reversing its emphasis. The champions of montage and the image have never known what to do about sound. Most resisted it initially; a few – like Arnheim – continue to despise it as a 'radical aesthetic impoverishment';[28] many have accepted it, if kept strictly in its place:

even with sound, the film remains primarily a visual art, and the major problem of technique with which film-makers should be pre-occupied today is that of finding a style which will combine the best elements of the silent film with the particular attributes of sound.[29]

In fact, this definition of the image and the sound-track as distinct formal 'elements' was the source of the theorists' difficulty. Arnheim went furthest in this direction – image and sound were 'separate and complete structural forms'[30] – and was quite unable to reconcile the two:

The unity which exists in real life between the body and voice of a person would be valid in a work of art only if there existed between the two components a kinship much more intrinsic than their belonging together biologically.[31]

But from the moment we see film, with Bazin, as a method of capturing reality rather than as a 'visual art', the difficulty is resolved. The movie is seen to absorb natural or biological unities into its formal structure. The silent cinema is thus revealed as an incomplete medium: 'reality minus one of its elements'.[32] It becomes easy to answer Arnheim even at his most perverse: 'Psychologically, a stop of the dialogue is not perceived as an interruption of the auditory action, the way the disappearance of the image

27. ibid., p. 146.
28. Arnheim, *Film as Art*, p. 188.
29. Lindgren, *The Art of the Film*, pp. 94–5.
30. Arnheim, *Film as Art*, p. 170.
31. ibid., p. 167.
32. Bazin, op. cit., Vol. I, p. 135.

from the screen would interrupt the visual performance.'[33] This is very true and for a simple 'biological' reason: we are all able to keep quiet, but have not yet learned to make ourselves invisible.

Bazin's work performed an inestimable service by blasting a way through the orthodox impasse. Important artistic procedures which established theory had dismissed now became open to serious discussion. An appreciation of Stroheim, Renoir, and Welles, among others, was given a rational basis. Yet Bazin's analyses of theoretical misconceptions and stylistic virtues do not amount to a satisfactory theory. His strictly theoretical statements provide no basis for many of his tastes and sympathies as a critic. His view tends to the creation of a dogma just as constricting as the orthodoxy. The tendency was fully realized by Kracauer who argued himself into condemning both the period movie and the film of fantasy for their 'inherently uncinematic character'.[34]

Bazin too, despite the sophisticated caution with which he limited his general statements, believed in the superiority of a particular set of technical procedures. Thus in an article on Jean Renoir, which must be one of the finest achievements of film criticism, he writes:

> Renoir is the director who has best grasped the true nature of the screen and freed it from dubious analogies with painting and the theatre. In visual terms the screen is habitually equated with a picture-frame and, dramatically, with the proscenium. These parallels result in an organization of visual material whereby the image is composed in relation to the sides of the rectangle . . . But Renoir saw clearly that the screen was simply the counterpart of the camera's viewfinder and therefore not a frame [which would enclose all that exists to be seen] but its opposite: a mask whose function is as much to exclude reality as to reveal it [because it enforces selection from a scene which exists outside the camera's range of vision]; what it shows draws its value from what it conceals.[35]

This is accurate and illuminating about one aspect of Renoir's style. It is theoretically useful for its exposure of the orthodoxy's

33. Arnheim, *Film as Art*, p. 173.
34. Kracauer, op. cit., p. 79.
35. Bazin, *Cahiers du Cinéma*, No. 8, January 1952, p. 26.

compositional dogma. But it is false and restrictive as a general, binding definition of the screen's *true nature*. As long as the screen has limits it is surely the artist's privilege to decide whether to exploit its sides as 'mask' or 'frame'. His decision tells us much about his attitudes and methods but nothing about the quality of his grasp on the medium.

Bazin mistook his own critical vocation to the defence of realism for the 'true vocation of the cinema'. His theoretical statements threaten a purism of the *object* as narrow as that of the image. Despite Bazin's careful qualifications and disclaimers, realist theory becomes coherent only if we identify the cinema's 'essence' with a single aspect of the film – photographic reproduction. In defining the film by reference to one of its features it resembles the orthodoxy, as it does in making a criterion out of a preference for particular aspects of film technique. Both theories discriminate in favour of certain kinds of cinematic effect, in other words certain kinds of attitude given cinematic form. The image dogma would assess quality in terms of the artist's imposition of order on the chaotic and meaningless surface of reality. Object dogma would derive its verdict from his discovery of significance and order *in* reality. Each of these positions presupposes a philosophy, a temperament, a vision – terrain which the theorist should leave open for the film-maker to explore and present.

3 Technology and Technique

Film belongs in the first place to its inventors. It is appropriated by artists but at every stage in the creation and presentation of their work they are dependent upon, and often at the mercy of, the machine and its operators. As the movie cannot exist apart from its apparatus, a satisfactory definition of the medium's artistic nature depends on a full recognition of its technological base. By reviewing the cinema's mechanism we can hope to correct some inadequacies of available film theories. Orthodox theorists shun technology, except where it allows distortion, because of their eagerness to dissociate art from mechanics. Realist theories take account of the cinema's basis in photography but do not give enough weight to other, equally important, factors in the movie mechanism. Kracauer argues, for example, that the 'affinities' of photography are necessarily manifest in the movies. One of these affinities, he says, is to suggest endlessness ('a photograph . . . is in character only if it precludes the notion of completeness').[1] There is some truth in this: a still photograph is literally an arrested development which can only suggest the events occurring before or after the film was exposed, or beyond the camera's range. Movies, however, can follow the event through and chart the development which the still photograph ignores. A film may be complete in a way which is not open to photography. It is invalid to argue from the properties of photography that 'cinematic films invoke a reality more inclusive than the one they actually picture'.[2]

Bazin and Kracauer share the view that film is 'essentially an extension of photography'[3] and that as a result 'the nature of

1. Kracauer, *Theory of Film*, p. 19.
2. ibid., p. 71.
3. ibid., p. ix.

photography survives in that of film'.[4] The position is taken for granted, not argued; it is both theoretically misleading and historically false. Movies owe their existence to a peculiarly mixed marriage between the camera, the magic lantern and the optical toys of the nineteenth century. The first magic lantern was demonstrated about 1660 and thus antedates the first successful attempts at photography by more than a century and a half. Magic lantern shows provided the earliest approximation to cinema: the use of superimposed slides provided an illusion of movement as, for example, a night scene dissolved into a daylight one. Slides containing a moving part were developed at the end of the nineteenth century in order to tell simple stories.

The investigation of the 'magical' possibilities of persistence of vision paralleled the development of photography. Niepce took his first photographs in the 1820s; in 1824 Dr P. M. Roget published his paper 'Persistence of Vision with regard to Moving Objects'. Optical toys based on this principle began to appear shortly afterwards. The first, manufactured in 1826, was a flat disc with a picture on each side; spinning the disc made the pictures seem to merge. This simple toy was described by its makers as a 'Thaumatropical Amusement. To illustrate the seeming paradox of Seeing an Object which is Out of Sight and to demonstrate the faculty of the Retina of the eye to retain the impression of an object after its disappearance'. In 1832 there appeared a new toy, the Phenakistascope, which made more sophisticated use of the principles formulated by Roget; a series of drawings, depicting separate stages in an action, was printed on a cardboard disc. Rotated, and viewed in a mirror through slots in its circumference, the Phenakistascope disc provided the first genuine moving pictures.

Other toys – the Heliocinegraphe (1850), the Zoetrope (1860), and the Praxinoscope Theatre (1877) – used the same basic method as the Phenakistascope but refined its mechanism. Reynaud, the inventor of the Praxinoscope, devised a machine to combine his toy with the magic lantern. Using drawings printed on a long roll of paper instead of the usual short and repetitious strip, Reynaud's

4. ibid., p. 27.

'Théâtre Optique' presented a moving picture show to a large audience. This, the earliest form of cinema, was quite independent of photography.

Thus the cinema is a device which creates an illusion of movement as much as it is an 'extension of photography'. Every method of using film presupposes movement, but there are movies – in particular certain forms of cartoon – which do not involve photography. The invention of the cine-camera was the *final* stage in the development which formed the prehistory of the movies. Thirty years before the camera was able to take the rapid series of pictures needed in order to analyse actual movement, photographs had been incorporated into various forms of optical toy. In 1861 William Thomas Shaw had exhibited his Stereotrope which used eight still photographs, taken with a stationary object in eight slightly different positions, as a means of simulating movement. Later inventions, like the Phantasmatrope and the Zoöpraxinoscope combined the animated photograph with the magic lantern.

The first technically and commercially viable movie camera was demonstrated in 1892 by W. K. L. Dickson, working in the laboratories of Thomas Edison; its product was viewed in the 'kinetoscope', a peep-show which enabled a fifty-foot loop of film to be seen by one customer at a time. European inventors, notably R. W. Paul and the Lumière brothers, devised projection systems for the Kinetoscope films and subsequently invented their own cine-camera. On 28 December 1895 the Lumière brothers presented movies to the public on a commercial basis for the first time, at the Grand Café in Paris.

In its conception and at its birth, the motion picture was a curious hybrid: the magic lantern was crossed with the optical toy, and the offspring of this liaison was mated with the camera. The cinema bears to this day (and for the foreseeable future) every mark of its mixed parentage. The relationship between illusion and reality is usually ambiguous and often chaotically muddled. The photographic film presents an intermittent pattern of coloured light but deludes us into seeing a continuous record of reality. In his 'History of the Kinematograph, Kinetoscope and Kinetophonograph' (1895) W. K. L. Dickson described the moving picture as 'an object of magical wonder, the crown and flower of nineteenth-century magic'.[5] In fact, every film-maker is an illusionist, exploiting persistence of vision as a necessary substitute for the conjurer's sleight of hand. In both cases, the quickness of the movement deceives the eye.

The projector's magic is fundamental to the movie's mechanical nature and should not be given less weight than the camera's special relationship with reality. Whenever we talk of the movie's realism we are discussing its artifice as well. It is possible to see the camera as no more than the most *convenient* machine that exists to produce the kinds and quantity of still images required by the projector. Conversely, as soon as we recognize the screen image as an illusion *derived* from reality we have to acknowledge the importance of the movie's photographic aspect.

The development of the cinema's technology shows the interdependence of realism and illusion. A device which animates pictures can do so whether the pictures are monochrome or coloured. Projectors were equipped from the outset to present colour movies, but had to wait forty years for the camera to record them. On the other hand there is no difficulty at the camera's end about recording reality so as to meet the requirements for three-dimensional reproduction. But a convenient method of stereoscopic projection has still to be devised. Increases in realism are necessarily extensions of illusion.

Despite imperfect synchronization of developments in recording and presentation, technology has propelled the cinema steadily towards increased realism. Film has been equipped to capture more aspects of reality and to interpose fewer of its own characteristics between audience and image so that the man in front of the screen comes ever nearer to seeing as much and as clearly as the man beside the camera. Changes in the extent of the cinema's realism are easy to chart since they depend on simple additions to its representation of the world: add sound, add colour, extend the screen horizontally, and the movie, 1895 model, comes substantially up to date. Changes in the quality of the cinema's realism are

5. Quoted in Jacobs, *The Rise of the American Film – A Critical History*, p. 4.

less abrupt and therefore less often noticed; but they are scarcely less important. They have tended to reduce distortion and interference and to increase flexibility so that movies become both more 'accurate' and more subject to control by their makers.

The speed with which the cinema evolves can change even the significance of its vocabulary. In the first decades of this century, the 'raw' film stocks available were very insensitive; strong light was needed in order to obtain a picture. Also, the film was 'colour blind': it registered light and dark but ignored the subtler tonal variations. When scientists devised a film stock more sensitive to green and yellow light than its predecessors, the manufacturers proudly called it Orthochrome to distinguish it from the less sensitive brands. However, in 1924–5 Panchromatic film came on the market; since this was sensitive to all colours and capable of reproducing them in the corresponding shades of black, grey or white, it was soon established as the normal film to use. Thereafter the word 'Orthochrome' came to denote a film of *inferior* sensitivity.

If we see changes of this kind as improvements in the cinema's technology, we presuppose a goal which is more nearly approached at each stage in the progress of the mechanism. In fact, changes in film technology have all tended in one direction: towards completing the illusion of reality. 'Since their inception,' says Jacobs, 'all progress in movies has been towards achieving a more effective reality.'[6] Even Arnheim, who resists the cinema's progress, does not deny its goal: 'the [engineer's] ideal is exactly to imitate real life'.[7]

This ideal is still a long way from realization, and may never be realized. It would demand a stereoscopic image effectively infinite in height and width. Most problematic of all, it would need to hold in the one image those variations of brightness which present technology requires the camera to compensate but forbids it to record. If the spectator is to receive no visual evidence that he is looking at an image, the illusion will have to survive inspection by eyes which retain in the 'cinema' the freedoms to which they are

6. ibid., p. 448.
7. Arnheim, *Film as Art*, p. 61.

accustomed in reality. This 'total cinema' would realize what Bazin called 'the myth directing the cinema's invention'[8] and fulfil M. L. Gunzburg's prophecy that 'audiences will come to watch a motion picture performance as though the screen were eliminated entirely and life itself unfolded'.[9]

Speculations about total cinema are entirely hypothetical. Yet they are also justified by the mechanical evolution of the movies in the past seventy years. To date, each of the major advances in film technology has been anticipated in the early history, and pre-history, of the cinema. Edison's Kinetophone provided a crude form of talkie. The animated images in Reynaud's Praxinoscope Theatre were presented in colour. Each of the sixteen tiny pictures projected in one second of Méliès's silent films was hand-tinted in his workshop in order to add colour to the black and white image: ten minutes' running time demanded nearly ten thousand separately painted frames, for each print of the film. As movies grew longer and expanding distribution increased the demand for prints, Méliès's method became impractical. The silent movie attempted to compensate for the absence of natural colour by immersing whole lengths of film in dye, so that the monochrome picture took on a tint 'appropriate' to the mood and setting of each sequence: green for countryside, blue for night-time and so on.

Experiments in direct colour cinematography date back to the beginning of the century. But it was not until Technicolor introduced its three-colour process in 1935 that an acceptable degree of fidelity and control began to be attainable. The ideal conception of a cinema complete with natural sound and colour certainly preceded the invention of the means by which this conception could be realized.

Similarly, in the late twenties, Magnascope and the 'grandeur screen' evidenced a desire to extend the screen and involve the audience more completely in its illusion. Both processes disappeared as a result of technical deficiencies, but the underlying

8. Bazin, *Qu'est-ce que le Cinéma?*, Vol. I, p. 25.
9. Quoted in Roger Manvell, *The Film and the Public*, Penguin Books, 1955, p. 102.

principle was the same as that which motivated the introduction of Cinemascope and the other wide-screen systems in the fifties.

The Cinerama process used three cameras and three projectors to engulf the spectator in its image; it was anticipated in 1927 by Abel Gance's experiment with a three-screen system for his film *Napoleon*. Earlier still, in 1900, Parisian spectators had been treated to a demonstration of 'Cinéorama' in which a circular screen surrounded them with views photographed from a balloon. Total cinema's predicted immersion of the spectator into an artificially complete environment has been foreshadowed: 'Hale's Tours', at the turn of the century, offered their customers seats in a rocking railway carriage; views of the passing scenery, taken from a moving train, were projected on to the 'observation window'.

Three-dimensional photography preceded the invention of the cine-camera. Its illusion of depth depends on an arrangement whereby each of the viewer's eyes accepts only one of two images photographed from slightly different angles. The difficulties involved in this process have so far prevented the establishment of the stereoscopic film on a lasting commercial basis. But the desire to produce moving pictures in three dimensions has been manifest since, at latest, 1890, when the English inventors Friese-Greene and Varley patented a stereoscopic cine-camera (of dubious efficiency). Short three-dimensional movies were introduced in the thirties. Like children's 3-D picture books they required the use of red and green tinted spectacles. In 1953 the Natural Vision process employed polarized spectacles to present 3-D films in colour, notably Hitchcock's *Dial M for Murder* and André de Toth's *House of Wax*. Once again, after scarcely more than a year's run, the three-dimensional movie was abandoned on account of its mechanical imperfections. It was inconvenient to project and, for most people, uncomfortable to watch.

We can expect the stereoscopic movie to continue making spasmodic appearances until its technical problems are finally resolved; the point is that we are already aware of its absence as an imperfection in the movie mechanism. Bazin pointed out that the cinema has always fallen short of the 'integral realism' which its inventors conceived but could not capture: 'paradoxically, all the refinements which have been added to the cinema can only bring it closer to its origins. The cinema has not yet been invented.'[10]

The concept of progress has a special significance for the movie which cannot be paralleled in other forms. It demands both respect and caution from the theorist since the cinema's image has always excluded more elements of reality than it has presented. If we are to relate critical judgements sensibly to mechanical development, we must discover the extent to which an imperfect technology imposes artistic limitations; we must also assess the ways in which such limitations can aid or obstruct various kinds of artistic communication.

In these respects the primitive technology of the silent cinema is instructive. Its silence was an historical and technical accident. Edison originally started his research into the possibilities of the moving photograph in order to provide a visual accompaniment for his other invention, the phonograph. The first movie demonstrated by Dickson was a short film, linked to the phonograph, in which he both appeared and spoke.

Until the late twenties when the sound film became both technically viable and commercially necessary, orchestral scores for the large-scale silent movies demanded an entire battery of realistic effects, from horses' hooves to pistol shots, designed to replace the sounds which the film itself could not provide. At its crudest, the silent picture made extensive use of printed titles in order to let the audience know not only what was being said (though many of the most devoted movie fans apparently became expert lip-readers), but also what was happening in the image. Silent movies seldom depended, except for comic effect, on mime – a style of acting which would have been appropriate if the absence of sound had been more than a technical accident. In fact when actors came closest to using mime, the exaggerated style of performance clashed with the realistic appearance of the image and produced a grotesque effect: the image made sense on the assumption that all the characters were deaf mutes, but this assumption was contradicted by other aspects of the action.

10. Bazin, op. cit., Vol. I, p. 25.

The limitations imposed by silence were complicated by the shortcomings of the image. Until the end of the cinema's second decade, film was slow and lighting equipment clumsy. Except in brightly sunlit exteriors, depth of focus was severely limited: in the studio either foreground or background objects could be sharply focused, but seldom both at the same time. The cameraman had to devote himself to obtaining a comprehensible picture; there was little opportunity to use lighting for subtle dramatic effects. During the twenties the advent of Panchromatic film, and improvements in lenses and lighting devices began to encourage refinements in set design and a more controlled use of variations in shade and texture.

In the meantime, film technique developed under severe mechanical restraints. If it was necessary to present a scene with more than two or three characters, the camera had to stand back from the action (in a 'long shot') in order to accommodate the actors within the frame. But then the definition of the image was not sharp enough to register clearly details of action, gesture or expression which were equally essential to the scene. It became necessary to isolate these details in separate close-ups. The immobility of the camera, which was again due to mechanical factors, usually made it impossible to travel continuously from long shot into close-up. The separate shots had to be joined by direct cuts from one position to another. With exceptions (like the one quoted from *Tih Minh*) rare enough to be startling, the standard method of breaking a scene down into separate shots of its various components, and reconstructing it in the cutting rooms, was not just convenient; it was essential if even relatively uncomplicated actions were to remain comprehensible.

On the other hand, mechanically imposed limitations often acted as a spur to the film-maker's inventiveness. There was then, as since, a constant two-way traffic between science and style, technology and technique. Early in his career D. W. Griffith became impatient with the uncontrolled floodlighting which his cameramen, Marvin and Bitzer, following accepted practice, declared to be necessary in order to secure an image. Then, according to Lewis Jacobs's account, Griffith deliberately chose a story that involved a problem in lighting, *The Drunkard's Reformation*. In one scene the actors were to be illuminated by a fireside glow. The cameramen protested that the film would not take an image if they followed Griffith's directions – or that the peculiar lighting would cast ugly shadows on the players' faces. But Griffith disdained all their objections, and Marvin and Bitzer photographed the scene under his direction. Projected the next day in the studio, the scene was greeted with a murmur of admiration, and the cameramen were perhaps the most surprised and approving of all. From then on lighting was regarded more seriously as a means of enhancing the dramatic effect of a film story.[11]

Similarly, Murnau's *The Last Laugh* (1924) adopted a revolutionary approach to the problems and possibilities of camera movement. But the revolution was inspired by the scriptwriter Carl Mayer as much as by the development of new machinery for transporting the camera. When *The Last Laugh* was still in the script stage, Mayer went to the photographer Karl Freund to find out how far it was possible to film long sections of the film with a continuously mobile camera. When Freund satisfied him that it could be done, Mayer started writing afresh and constructed his screenplay to exploit the possibilities to the full. A year earlier, Mayer's insistence on extending the mobility of the camera had obliged the photographer Guido Seeber to devise a tripod which moved on rails in order to carry out the requirements of Mayer's screenplay for *New Year's Eve*. For *The Last Laugh*, again at Mayer's instigation, Murnau was supplied with a fully automatic camera, which provided a high degree of mobility.

Although it required improvements in technology, Mayer's preoccupation with camera movement was not itself technological. It came out of his desire to intensify the dramatic effect of the silent picture and to make the image more expressive. The movements in *The Last Laugh* help to build the emotional pressure, to heighten the audience's response by involving it more closely with the characters. In this respect, Mayer's use of camera movement resembles the development of the close-up, and of editing, by Griffith.

11. Jacobs, op. cit., p. 104.

Initially, as we have seen, the close-up was necessary because it was impossible to present details clearly within their settings; and as soon as a picture began to be built up from isolated details, editing was automatically involved. The film-maker's freedom of choice operated with this mechanically imposed framework: he was able to select those details which seemed most significant and to determine their place within the total structure. In this way the need to show an event clearly gave rise to another means of influencing the audience's reaction, and thus of communicating the film-maker's own vision. As he developed his editing methods Griffith exploited the freedom of movement *between* shots, by varying their relationship in time and space, and thus compensated for restrictions on movement *within* the shots. But his style provided more than a simple compensation. The details which he chose to show and the rhythms of his editing contributed to his films' dramatic and emotional impact. Pudovkin quoted one sample, from *Intolerance* (1916), in his *Film Technique*:

> There is a scene in which a woman hears the death sentence passed on her husband, who is innocent of the crime. The director shows the face of the woman: an anxious, trembling smile through tears. Suddenly the spectator sees for an instant her hands, only her hands, the fingers convulsively gripping the skin. This is one of the most powerful moments in the film. Not for a minute did we see the whole figure, but only the face, and the hands.[12]

In the first thirty years of movies, style was governed primarily by efforts to make the unsupported image do all the work. Film-makers had to elaborate their portrayal of actions and reactions in order to achieve a comprehensible narrative. Some, like Griffith, were able to exploit this necessity so that the means employed to make the action clear became the means also of 'directing' its impact and significance. Applied without the skill or tact of a Griffith, however, elaboration tended to burden rather than support the picture. The presentation of events often became clumsy and repetitive. The momentum of the action could easily

12. Pudovkin, *Film Technique and Film Acting*, p. 93.

be lost in a strenuous pursuit of clarity by mediocre directors, or of effect and meaning by ambitious ones.

A very narrow range of relationships and situations can be investigated on film without examining the content of speech. Within the range, verbal communication is either unnecessary (as between Keaton and cannon) or so direct and naïve (as between Laurel and Hardy) that its content is effectively conveyed by action, grimace and gesture. Lindsay noted the silent picture's partiality for fights and chases, and its tendency to 'hurry through to what would be tremendous passions on the stage to recover something that can be really photographed'.[13] The medium was most manageable where plot, theme and genre combined to encourage elaboration at the level of pure action, as in the comedies of Chaplin, Keaton, and Laurel and Hardy or the melodramas of Feuillade and Fritz Lang. At their best, these films had nothing missing and nothing superfluous They were neither undernourished nor overweight but derived all they needed from the resources of the speechless image. They achieved something like perfection within the available range.

But where the silent movie went much beyond that range it laboured mightily. It faced a choice between clarity and economy whenever it dealt with situations, relationships, motives and responses which could not be expressed in direct, physical action. At such points the film-maker was forced back on to cumbersome paraphrases by means of printed titles, dumb-show or grandiose symbolism. The aspiration to subtlety and complexity might be implicit in the choice of subject, but it was all too often undermined by the crude and laboured quality of the devices which made the subject comprehensible.

The sound film's innovation was not the talking picture but the audible picture. Its arrival improved the medium, as distinct from the mechanism, in the sense that it greatly enlarged the range of communicable subjects, treatments and attitudes. Depth and complexity became compatible with economy over an enormously wider field once the presentation of events ceased to demand elaborate processes of exposition. From this point of view, the

13. Lindsay, *The Art of the Moving Picture*, p. 43.

addition of the sound-track represents less a necessary move towards 'realism' as such than a vitally significant extension of the
medium's formal opportunities.

But the crudities of early sound equipment were such as to put a
cruel emphasis on the film-maker's subjection to his apparatus.
The camera, so recently given freedom of movement, was put back
in chains: the noise of its motor had to be confined within a sound-
proof box. Set-designers were hamstrung by the requirements of
the microphone: the shape of the décor and the materials used in
its construction were dictated by the need to avoid 'dead spots'
and reverberation. The microphone itself was unselective and
picked up every sound it was offered – the creaking of the hero's
shoes or the heroine's corset as well as the dialogue which was
meant to reach the audience. William DeMille, now a film director,
commented:

> At present the main struggle is to perfect a craft upon which the future
> art may be founded . . . However amusing it may be to theorize on the
> future development of the Talkie, the real problem which confronts us
> in the studios today is the actual production of the thing itself . . . It is
> not the sound expert who makes the trouble – it is the sound itself.
> Modern directors are as dependent upon their 'Mixers' as they have
> always been on their cameramen.[14]

The problems with which sound confronted the film-makers
were many and complex. But they were quickly mastered. Refinements in recording technique quickly made the microphone as
flexible as the camera had been at the end of the silent era; mobility
was restored. The theorist's predicament was more acute and less
readily surmounted. The talking picture called in question the
whole structure of aesthetic judgement which analysis and speculation had created for the silent film.

Orthodox theorists had set out to vindicate the artistic integrity
of the silent picture. They had centred their appeal on mechanical
limitations as a guarantee of 'difference from reality'. They could
see no way for Art to survive if the most obvious and formative of
the limitations were removed. Their system of judgement placed

14. Quoted by John Scotland, *The Talkies*, Technical Press, London,
1930, pp. 181–2.

the highest value on precisely those devices which translated verbal statements into images. The composed image, the close-up and montage had become sanctified as the essential means of artistic expression. Sound threatened them with redundancy.

A poor future was forecast for the talkie. 'If the Vitaphone gets its deadly hold on the movies,' George Jean Nathan predicted, 'it won't be long before the latter's current millionaires are driven back to their former pants and delicatessen businesses.'[15] From an aesthetic rather than economic point of view Rotha was equally gloomy: sound, and other extensions to the cinema's realism, meant that 'gradually the powerful resources of cutting and editing will be forgotten and instead there will be long scenes lasting for minutes'.[16] Rotha failed to observe that with sound 'long scenes lasting for minutes' had a greater chance of achieving significance than the silent movie had given them. Where the sound film was thought to be admissible at all, it was on condition that it obeyed the rules drawn up for its speechless predecessor. Sound was to become a further element in the montage structure. Balazs followed the general line in ruling that

only when the sound film will have resolved noise into its elements, segregated individual, intimate voices and made them speak to us separately in vocal, acoustic close-ups; when these isolated detail sounds will be collated again in purposeful order by sound-montage, will the sound film have become a new art.[17]

The pattern established with the arrival of the sound film has been repeated with each extension of the cinema's realism. At each stage in the movie's development film-makers devise specific methods of overcoming, and exploiting, their limitations. But the theorist canonizes those methods and resents the removal of the limitation which made them necessary. 'Engineers,' says Arnheim,

are not artists. They do not direct their efforts toward providing the artist with a more effective medium, but toward increasing the natural-ness of film pictures ... They want to keep on getting nearer to nature

15. Nathan, *Art of the Night*, p. 135.
16. Rotha, *The Film Till Now*, p. 402.
17. Balazs, *Theory of the Film*, p. 198.

and do not realize that they thereby make it increasingly difficult for film to be art ... What might be called the 'drawbacks' of film technique (and which engineers are doing their best to 'overcome') actually form the tools of the creative artist.[18]

Established film theory is distinguished by its reverence for the drawbacks, its insistence on the beneficent nature of mechanical limitations. According to Manvell, 'it is wrong to try to make art too life-like: it becomes released from its limitations and so loses its sense of form and proportion'. 'All works of art,' he says, 'are successful because of, not in spite of, the limitations their form imposes on them.'[19] Lindgren's attitude is identical: 'The competent artist will regard the natural limitations of his medium rather as sources of opportunity than as irksome restraints.'[20]

The idea that form and style are made possible by the observance of limitations is common to most theories of art. But theory must distinguish a discipline freely accepted by the artist from inhibitions dictated by external forces. Restraints imposed on the filmmaker by mechanical contingencies are not helpfully defined as 'the natural limitations of his medium', even when those restraints are most artfully exploited. As the cinema has absorbed more aspects of reality it has increased the film-maker's powers of selection. Nothing since the introduction of the talkie has yielded (or can be expected to yield) so vast an increase in the range of experience accessible to the cinema. But other technological refinements have extended both the film-maker's freedom to select an appropriate form and his control within the form selected.

Only with colour as an available resource can we regard the use of black-and-white photography as the result of an artistic decision. Only in the sound film can a director use silence for dramatic effect. Jean-Luc Godard's decision to make *Les Carabiniers* (1963) look as if it had been photographed on Orthochrome stock gained its significance from the rejected possibility of achieving a clearer and more 'modern' image. In *Dr Strangelove*, Stanley Kubrick showed us our planet's atomic destruction in the third world war

18. Arnheim, *Film as Art*, pp. 61, 69, 109.
19. Manvell, *Film*, pp. 27, 28.
20. Lindgren, *The Art of the Film*, p. 53.

to the accompaniment of a popular song ('We'll meet again, don't know where, don't know when . . .'): we could be sure that he intended the ironic effect. No such confidence was possible in Lindsay's day; in Springfield, 1915, he complained,

the local moving picture managers think it necessary to have orchestras . . . With fathomless imbecility, hoochey koochey strains are on the air while heroes are dying. The Miserere is in our ears when the lovers are reconciled. Ragtime is imposed upon us while the old mother prays for her lost boy.[21]

Hitchcock's two versions of his thriller *The Man Who Knew Too Much* demonstrate the increase in artistic possibilities yielded by extensions of the cinema's realism. The original, released in 1934, was in black and white; the 1956 remake was in colour. The climax of both versions occurs during a concert in the Albert Hall: at a predetermined point in the performance of the 'Storm Cloud Cantata' an important foreign statesman is to be assassinated. Only one woman in the audience knows of the plot and can prevent the assassination. But her child has been kidnapped in order to secure her silence. The sequence is built on the conflict between the demands of conscience (prevention of the murder) and those of instinct (the safe return of the child). It is essential in both versions that we remain continuously aware of the mother's anxiety for the fate of her child, while the other side of the conflict is most actively present on the screen. Both versions therefore employ a device to represent the woman's concern. In the earlier film, this device is obvious to the point of crudity. The mother clutches a badge which belonged to her child. A close-up of her hand gripping the badge is inserted to remind us of the price of intervention. Hitchcock's use of colour in the remake creates a more subtle effect. Throughout the picture the child is associated with the colour red. Once inside the auditorium of the Albert Hall, the threat to the child is represented by the bright red drapes which play an obtrusive, but natural, part in the images. Hitchcock no longer needs to stress an unlikely symbol when he can show the assassin hiding behind red curtains in order to take aim. This image is more directly symbolic

21. Lindsay, op. cit., pp. 219–20.

of the relationship between the child and the conspiracy than any
in the earlier film; but it is integrated into the design of the
sequence. In the 1934 version the detail has to be interpreted before
it can create its emotional effect. The more subtle procedure made
possible by colour allows Hitchcock to bypass the intellectual
response and go straight to the emotions. The spectator does not
have to *translate* the use of colour, as he must the use of the badge,
in order to be affected by it.

It is important to note that the addition of colour to the
director's resources allows, but does not impose, the more subtle
effect. Hitchcock could still have chosen to include the device with
the badge in colour film. In this respect also the two pictures
demonstrate the impact of technology on technique. Devices
which are necessitated by one set of mechanical limitations become
optional, but not unusable, when those limitations are removed.

Since the early forties, increases in clarity, depth of focus and
screen area have encouraged the tendency towards a more complex
and fluid camera style. The wide screen, in particular, extended the
film-maker's resources for the organization of action within a
single shot. Consequently directors became much less dependent
on cutting than they were in the thirties. But Cinemascope and the
other wide-screen systems did not, as their antagonists predicted,
deprive film-makers of the resources of editing. On the contrary,
the more fluid presentation encouraged by the 'scope screen gave
added weight to passages of staccato cutting like those in Nicholas
Ray's *Rebel Without a Cause* and to the shattered continuities of
Alain Resnais's *Last Year in Marienbad*. Devices can be moulded
into a style only when they have become inessential and, in the
most favourable sense, gratuitous. In any medium, style is formed
by a pattern of decisions; but decisions can operate only where
alternatives exist.

The more completely the cinema is able to duplicate 'mere
reality', the wider becomes the range of alternatives open to the
film-maker. The flexibility of the medium is the freedom of the
artist. While an increase in the area of reality available to the film-
maker extends the possibility of *choice*, mechanical refinements
also extend the opportunities for *control*, within each area.

The orthodox conviction that mechanical improvements 'seek to achieve the realism so antagonistic to an imaginative medium'[22] ignores the interdependence of imagination and accuracy, reality and illusion. The attempt to show 'how the very properties that make photography and film fall short of perfect reproduction can act as the necessary moulds of an artistic medium'[23] puts the emphasis in the wrong place, by making temporary limitations of the cinema's mechanism stand in for a coherent view of its *artistic* disciplines. This attitude can produce only a series of negative criteria. 'Editing is . . . the intrinsic essence of filmic creation'[24] really means: Thou shalt not present without cuts long scenes lasting for minutes.

As technology develops, its control over technique becomes less pronounced. The more the cinema moves towards the 'art without limitations' predicted by Eisenstein, the more important it becomes to relate our criteria to inherent possibilities rather than imposed restrictions. Standards derived primarily from the 'demands of the medium' have proved unsatisfactory partly because the medium has become less and less demanding, but also because the demands attributed to the medium are necessarily the *critic's* demands in an unhelpful disguise.

Arnheim asserts that 'an essential condition of a good work of art is that the special attributes of the medium employed should be clearly and cleanly laid bare'.[25] In Rotha's book, 'a film requires the theme to be emphasized by the full range of cinematic resources'.[26] But the movie's special attributes are so contradictory as to resist clear and clean definition. The full range of cinematic resources is so wide that the use of one device precludes the use of others which are equally cinematic. Montage is certainly a special attribute of the movies; but no less special is the possibility of recording a long sequence of actions in strict continuity, either from a fixed viewpoint or with a mobile camera. These contra-

22. Rotha, op. cit., p. 110.
23. Arnheim, *Film as Art*, p. 13.
24. Rotha, op. cit., Ch. 1, ref. 50.
25. Arnheim, *Film*, p. 46.
26. Rotha, op. cit., p. 338.

dictory resources stand in the way of the attempt to equate Cinema with a particular method of using film.

The search for grace through purity contradicts the cinema's hybrid character. It attempts to reduce the movie to one of its functions. In part a recording mechanism but also an optical illusion, an art based on reality but dependent also on magic, the film is inherently impure; its facilities are too varied and too much in conflict to be absorbed within a single technical formula. At the same time, the movie's mutually exclusive possibilities are essential to the fact of choice and the concept of style.

4 Form and Discipline

I do not believe that the film (or any other medium) has an essence which we can usefully invoke to justify our criteria. We do not deduce the standards relevant to Rembrandt from the essence of paint; nor does the nature of words impose a method of judging ballads and novels. Standards of judgement cannot be appropriate to a medium as such but only to particular ways of exploiting its opportunities. That is why the concept of the cinematic, presented in terms of demands, has stunted the useful growth of film theory. Helpful criteria are more likely to be based on positive statements of value than on prohibitions. To regard criticism positively, as a search for the most satisfactory definitions of function and value, allows an escape from academic systems of rules and requirements. Criteria then relate to claims which the critic can sustain rather than to demands which he must make. The clarification of standards should help to develop the disciplines of criticism without seeking to lay obligations on the film-maker. Criticism and its theory are concerned with the interplay of available resources and desirable functions. They attempt to establish what the medium is good for. They cannot determine what is good for the medium, because the question is senseless. The search for appropriate criteria leads us to observe limitations; it does not allow us to prescribe them. Anything possible is also permissible, but we still have to establish its value. We cannot assess worth without indicating function.

Hence we can evolve useful criteria only for specific types of film, not for the cinema. Our standards of judgement will have to follow from definitions of types in terms of both their possibilities and their limitations. We have to discover what values we can claim for, what functions it makes sense to assign to, particular applications of the moving picture's resources. Our major concern will be with the different opportunities which can be realized within the various forms of cinema. A theory of film which claims universal validity must provide either an exhaustive catalogue of film forms or a description of the medium in such general terms as to offer minimal guidance to the appreciation of any movie. The problem arises from the embarrassing richness of the cinema's aptitudes.

The movie offers two forms of magic, since its conquest of the visible world extends in two opposite directions. The first, on which the realist theory concentrates, gives it the power to 'possess' the real world by capturing its appearance. The second, focus of the traditional aesthetic, permits the presentation of an ideal image, ordered by the film-maker's will and imagination. Since the cinema's mechanism incorporates both these tendencies, neither of them can be condemned on rational, technical or aesthetic grounds. A useful film theory must acknowledge the range and diversity of the film-maker's achievements. At one end of the scale we find the most rigorous forms of documentary, which aim to present the truth about an event with the minimum of human intervention between the real object and its film image; at the other end lies the abstract, cartoon or fantasy film which presents a totally controlled vision. This diversity of methods might be attributed to the movies' mixed parentage, the 'objective', factual elements being derived from the camera and the 'subjective', magical ones from the Phenakistascope and its relations.

Within the first few years of the cinema's existence the polarities were firmly established. The Lumière brothers' first movie-show presented short 'actualities' – a train entering a station, baby eating breakfast and so on. In the 'earliest days the fact that a machine could present real situations in recognizable form was sufficient sensation to draw enthusiastic audiences throughout Europe and the United States. As soon as that magic lost its appeal, Georges Méliès was ready to step in with the other kind. A professional magician, Méliès took up film-making in 1896 and devoted himself to exploiting the cinema as a medium for fantasy. Using every form of camera trickery he could invent, he told a series of amusing and amazing stories. His two most famous pictures, *A Trip to the Moon* (1902) and *The Impossible Voyage* (1904), presented fantastic situations in fantastic settings. They are packed with magical appearances, disappearances and transformations. The arrival of Méliès and the subsequent development of the narrative film revived the public's waning interest in motion pictures.

Lumière's actualities represent one extreme of the cinema and Méliès's fantasies are quite near to the other. But few films confine themselves to either a purely reproductive or a purely imaginative technique. The cinema extends across the whole of the area between the two extremes. The photographic narrative film occupies a compromise position where a fictional 'reality' is *created* in order to be *recorded*. Here the relationship between reality and illusion, object and image, becomes extremely complex; any attempt to isolate either in a 'pure' state becomes correspondingly inept.

The fiction movie exploits the possibilities of synthesis between photographic realism and dramatic illusion. That synthesis, its value and implications, will be the major subject of this study. Unless a wider relevance is explicitly claimed, the reader should assume that arguments are meant to apply only to the cinema of photographic fiction. I hope to present criteria which will aid discussion of various kinds and degrees of excellence within this form. I shall offer no case about the usefulness of other forms, nor will my remarks be relevant to the qualities of works outside the range of my definitions. The chosen field to some extent reflects the limits of my familiarity and enthusiasm, but that is all. It would clearly be possible and useful to argue claims and criteria for cartoon, documentary, instructional and many other kinds of film which lie beyond the scope of this study. Nonetheless the fiction movie presents the most urgent claim to attention for two reasons: by almost any reasonable method of calculation, it must be granted the central role in the cinema's development; but it is also precisely the fictional element which existing film theories have most difficulty in accommodating.

A necessary consequence of adopting positive criteria is that we are better equipped to praise than to condemn. Discriminations will be possible within the type, in so far as we see one film as a more complete or skilful realization of its opportunities than another. But the claims we can make for a comedy by Howard Hawks will not yield ammunition for use against an Ingmar Bergman allegory, because they belong to types almost as distinct as cartoon and documentary. Even within the field of cine-fiction the range of possibilities remains enormous. The critical problem is to arrive at descriptions which are both specific and comprehensive enough to be useful. The critic cannot require a movie to fit his definitions; it's his task to find the description which best fits the movie. The most he can 'demand' from a film is coherence: a structure which points consistently towards the performance of comprehensible functions. Without that, judgement becomes impossible. From this viewpoint the most significant limitations are those of the form rather than of the medium, the disciplines which the film-maker obeys in order to pursue a particular range of opportunities. For if there are no rules by which every movie can be bound, there are forms which, once adopted by the film-maker, impose their own logic both on him and on the intelligent spectator, since the opportunities of the form may be realized only at the expense of other, attractive but incompatible, possibilities. Yet the central issue remains: not what the film-maker may not do, but the value we can find in what he has done.

In a hybrid form the quest for purity is much less important than the achievement of an ideal compromise, a meaningful resolution of inherent conflict. The fictional film exploits, where purer forms attempt to negate, the conflict between reality and illusion. Instead of trying exclusively either to create or to record, the story film attempts a synthesis: it both records what has been created and creates by its manner of recording. At its most powerful it achieves a credibility which consummates the cinema's blend of actuality and fantasy.

The credibility of the movies comes, I believe, from our habit of placing more trust in the evidence of our eyes than in any other form of sense data: a film makes us feel like eye-witnesses of the events which it portrays. Moreover, our belief extends even to the least realistic forms of movie because movement so strongly connotes life. The source meaning of the term 'animation' indicates that we regard a moving picture, even a cartoon, as a picture *brought to life*. In the early days of the movies words like cinematograph and kinetoscope, which meant *moving* picture, were interchangeable with words meaning *living* picture (vitascope, biograph, bioscope, etc.). The powerful combination of picture and movement tempts us to disregard the involvement of our imaginations in what we see.

Of course, the degree and level of credibility varies from film to film and at different points within a single movie. In this respect Dusan Vukotic's *Play* is an exemplary picture. Two children are sitting on the floor surrounded by sheets of drawing paper. The little boy draws a car, the little girl a flower. The car comes to life, runs across the sheets of paper and destroys the flower. Boy and girl commence a battle of drawings: the boy draws a lion to chase the girl's doll; the girl draws a house as refuge for her doll and adds a rifle with which to shoot the lion. The conflict 'escalates' into a nuclear war (and a charming picture declines into a pretentious cold-war allegory). In his excitement, the boy spills a bottle of ink over the drawings (atomic destruction!) and the children fight. The film ends with them both in tears.

What matters here is not the film's debatable quality but its method and effect. The only rational explanation for its events is that the battle takes place in the children's minds; the animated parts would then fall into place as projections of their thoughts. But this is not the way the film works. The girl sees what we see: the boy's drawn car crushing her drawn flower. The story makes the children react as freely to the animated action as to the real events, and puts the real boy and girl on exactly the same level as the animated drawings. It makes sense only if we accept the flower's destruction as a real event, just like the accident with the ink. The film might be expected to irritate its audience by requiring simultaneous belief in actions which exist on two different levels of credibility. In fact the cinema's magic is powerful enough to overcome purely rational objections of this sort. Audiences enter into Vukotic's movie without apparent difficulty; it was only after I had seen the film for the third time that its mixture of reality and illusion (different kinds of illusion) began to seem at all strange.

The most 'realistic' films are the ones which convey the most complete illusion. The most obviously imaginative films, the 'pure works of man' – cartoons and fantasies – lean heavily upon the cinema's realistic resources in order to make us see the impossible and believe the incredible. When the cartoon cat walks confidently off the edge of a skyscraper and stands paralysed for a couple of fearful seconds before falling, it is precisely our habit of believing our eyes that makes a piece of anti-Newtonian nonsense amusing.

Some abstract films make no use of the cinema's realism (the spectator's credulity). They do not pretend to show real objects but are an extension of non-representational painting. Yet even films in this genre – like Norman McLaren's 'caprice in colour', *Begone, Dull Care* – seem to rely on our anthropomorphic tendencies. Whenever the opportunity arises movement becomes action (a round blob 'bumps into' a vertical line: accident or aggression?) and shape becomes object (a coloured circle: a ball, a wheel, the sun?). Ernest Pintoff's cartoon *The Critic* comments joyfully on the abstract film's tendency to shed its abstract quality. The screen is filled with coloured shapes which apparently defy interpretation. After a few seconds we hear a Bronx-accented voice demanding 'What the hell is this?' The question is momentarily resolved: 'Must be a cartoon.' Pause. Small blob emerges from 'inside' larger blob and the interpretation begins: 'Must be Birth.' The shapes are rearranged and the spectator becomes confused again: 'This is cute. This is cute. This is nice. What the hell *is* it?' Two black shapes converge from opposite sides of the screen: 'Two Things!... They like each other.' (Rhythmic movement of black shapes.) 'Could this be the sex life of two Things?' As the commentary progresses (spiky black oval: 'Uh-uh! It's a cockroach') it becomes increasingly contemptuous of the movie's imagined content ('Dirt! Dirt and filth!') until, after four minutes of 'pure' abstraction the critic reaches his conclusion: 'I don't know much about psychoanalysis, but I'd say this is a dirty picture.' Pintoff's movie is funny because it is accurate. With any luck actual spectators can be heard commenting and interpreting before 'the critic' starts to speak; the two sets of remarks are often very similar.

If abstract shapes in movement attract 'realistic' interpretation as objects and actions, it is hardly surprising that the moving photograph carries such conviction. Photographic subjects, says Newhall, 'can be misrepresented, distorted, faked ... and [we] even delight in it occasionally, but the knowledge still cannot shake our implicit faith in the truth of a photographic record'.[1]

In 1895 the Lumières' audience believed completely in the reality of a soundless, colourless, two-dimensional and rigidly enclosed image: the spectators feared for their lives when shown an oncoming train. Sixty years later, engulfed in Cinerama's huge screen and surrounded by a battery of realistic sound effects, people reacted to film taken from the front of a roller-coaster just as they would react to a ride on a real switchback. They gripped the arms of their seats, screamed and even felt the authentic stomach-tumbling effect. Still, we can hardly claim that *This Is Cinerama* offered a perfect illusion. Its picture, while not exactly flat, was less than three-dimensional. The joins between its three images were clearly visible. We were subjected to none of the physical effects essential to a total illusion: no wind disturbed the spectator's hair as he rode the switchback, no smell reached his nostrils as he was conducted along the canals of Venice.

But although Cinerama provided only a partial illusion, it imposed the only sort of belief which we can regard as truly complete: the audience was made to react to the image as it would to the event. The trick here is just the same as it was with the Lumières' presentation and with the 3-D films whose audiences dived for cover under a barrage of arrows, axes and ping-pong balls: not to provide a perfect illusion, that is an integral reproduction of reality, but to offer enough of reality to make the spectator disregard what is missing.

This kind and degree of belief is inevitably short-lived since 'enough' means 'more than ever before'. Audiences rapidly adjust to any extension of the cinema's realism. The primitive magic which creates belief in the real presence of the object shown soon loses its power. 'Illusion wears off once ... expectation is stepped

1. Newhall, *The History of Photography from 1839 to the Present Day*, p. 91.

up; we take it for granted and want more.'[2] After less than ten minutes of *This Is Cinerama* the sense of being transported around the world began to be replaced by a more conscious appreciation of the techniques by which the world was so convincingly brought into the cinema. The illusory environment of the roller-coaster or the Venetian canal is too inconsistent with what we know about our actual situation for a lasting deception.

But even if we do not believe in the actual presence of the things we see, a film remains credible so long as we are not led to question the *reality* of the objects and events presented. Verbal statements and propositions are seen as either true or false: if we believe them, we believe them; if not, not. Sights, sounds and, particularly, stories – the things which we believe *in* – present a much more complex problem. Belief here can occur in so many ways and at so many levels.

Films are often described as existing in the present tense. Like most direct linguistic analogies this one promotes confusion rather than enlightenment. It implies that we see a film as a series of events taking place for the first time. Usually we are well aware that this is not the case, just as we know that the conjurer has not magically transformed the queen of hearts into the king of spades. If films were really seen in the present tense cinema managers would have always to protect their screens against assault by gallant spectators rushing to the aid of embattled heroines. If we can describe the movie as existing in any tense at all then the nearest equivalent is probably the historic present which evokes the vividness of memory or fantasy: 'There I am walking along the street, and there's this old man standing on the corner. And then he steps out into the road just as this lorry comes round . . .'

Our reaction to the cinema, when we are not caught unawares by some new development like Cinerama or 3-D, is conditioned by our awareness that the camera is a recording instrument and the projected film a method of reproduction. Just as we can talk of hearing Bessie Smith on a gramophone record despite our knowledge that the singer is long dead, so we can watch events taking place on the screen *now* while remaining aware that they actually

2. E. H. Gombrich, *Art and Illusion*, Phaidon Press, 1962, pp. 53–4.

occurred some time ago. In both cases we accept the accuracy of the illusion.

Ideally the sounds coming from the gramophone's loudspeaker are indistinguishable from the sounds which first went into the microphone. Even when a recorded performance falls spectacularly short of this ideal we have great difficulty in disentangling the sounds made by the artist from the noises made by the recording: it is impossible to be certain how much our concept of what Bessie Smith sounded like is derived from tones which should be attributed to primitive recording mechanisms, not to the singer. Our belief in the recording is not shaken by our knowledge that the 'Bessie Smith sound' may not be a very faithful reproduction of the voice of Bessie Smith. It is hard not to feel, against reason, that the recording renders accurately the sounds made by the jazz-singer and her accompanists: if I ask myself to describe Bessie Smith's vocal quality, 'scratchy' is one of the words which most immediately comes to mind.

Similarly I find it hard to form a mental picture of life in the first decade of this century which does not include people walking faster and more jauntily than they do nowadays. The image offered by accelerated projection of early films takes mental precedence over the recognized unlikelihood of an evolution towards slower walking.

It is the belief in the actual (if past) existence of the objects on the screen which enables us to discuss movies in terms of credibility. Clearly, one cannot record something which has never existed. Everything that happens on the screen in a live-action picture has happened in front of the camera. The particular magic of the narrative film is to make us put an inaccurate construction on an accurate series of images. The camera neither lies nor tells the truth, because the camera does not make statements. It is we who convert images into assertions. The cinema shows us a man holding a pistol at his head, squeezing the trigger and falling to the floor. This is precisely what happened. But we fictionalize this documentary image when we claim to have seen a man committing suicide.

A more concrete example is offered by the film *Marilyn*. This 'tribute' to Marilyn Monroe was mainly composed of extracts from her films. The change of context, and hence of interpretation, converted the fictional images from such pictures as *Niagara*, *Gentlemen Prefer Blondes* and *River of No Return* into a documentary picture of an actress's career. *Gentlemen Prefer Blondes* showed us Lorelie Lee singing 'Diamonds Are a Girl's Best Friend' in a night-club. The same sequence of images leaves the realm of fiction when used in *Marilyn* to show us how the actress looked singing 'Diamonds . . .' in her role as Lorelie Lee in the film *Gentlemen Prefer Blondes*.

Since it exists only in the mind, in terms of the way in which we relate the image to reality, the distinction between authentic and fictional images is extremely fluid. Few people could see *Gentlemen Prefer Blondes* and remain unaware for any considerable period that Lorelie Lee is Marilyn Monroe. But when we see *Marilyn* it is equally difficult for us to stay outside the illusion and to resist false interpretations. Although *Marilyn* shows us only how Miss Monroe appeared in *Gentlemen Prefer Blondes*, we interpret it as showing us Marilyn Monroe singing a song. We may know that the sequence involved several days' work first in the recording studio and then in front of the cameras where the actress mimed to a carefully edited tape. It is still almost impossible not to believe that Marilyn Monroe sang 'Diamonds Are a Girl's Best Friend' in the way that we see and hear it. We can accept easily enough that 'Lorelie Lee' is a fiction. It is much less simple to reconcile ourselves to the fact that 'Marilyn Monroe' was an almost equally synthetic product. The 'true' *Marilyn* would have to show us Norma Jean Baker as Marilyn Monroe as Lorelie Lee. As it stands the film is a document about a myth.

The camera does not discriminate between real events (which would have taken place even if it had not been on the spot to record them) and action created specifically in order to be recorded. In this respect, the movie simply extends the ambiguity present in any credible image; so long as it looks correct we have no way of telling whether a picture portrays an actual or an imagined subject. The blurred distinction between authentic and staged events helps to make the cinema a peculiarly vivid medium. It is absurd to claim that movies are like life; but it is certain that they can impress us as being more lifelike than any other form of narrative.

The moving image lends its immediacy and conviction, its concreteness of credible detail, to the fictional world. But at this point the film-maker confronts the limitation that accompanies opportunity. If he chooses to exploit the credibility of the recording, he thereby sacrifices some of the freedom to invent and arrange which is offered by the celluloid strip. The discipline is inherent in the attempt to create from a succession of images an apparently solid world which exists in its own right.

In the fiction movie, reality becomes malleable but remains (or continues to seem) solid. The world is shaped by the film-maker to reveal an order beyond chronology, in a system of time and space which is both natural and synthetic. The movie offers its reality in a sequence of privileged moments during which actions achieve a clarity and intensity seldom found in everyday life. Motive and gesture, action and reaction, cause and effect, are brought into a more immediate, dynamic and revealing relationship. The film-maker fashions a world more concentrated and more shaped than that of our usual experience.

Movies are not distinguished from other forms of narrative by the fact that they isolate and mould aspects of experience in order to intensify our perception. But films are peculiar in performing this work primarily in the sphere of action and appearance rather than of reflection or debate.

The story-teller's freedom to create is inhibited by his two first requirements: clarity and credibility. In movies, the most direct and concrete method of narration, these aims impose a greater restraint than on any other medium. The audience has to know what is happening, of course, but it must also be convinced by what it sees. The organization of image and sound must usually defer to these interests. The narrative picture, in most of its forms, submits to the twin criteria of order and credibility. The movie itself creates these criteria whenever it proposes to be at the same time significant and convincing. The impurity of the medium is consummated by a decision to project a world which is both reproduced and imagined, a creation and a copy. Committed to this impurity, the film-maker is also committed to maintaining a balance between its elements. His aim is to organize the world to the point where it becomes most meaningful but to resist ordering it out of all resemblance to the real world which it attempts to evoke.

Since stories do not exist except as they are told, and since film worlds can be discussed only as they are seen and shown, to discuss the opportunities available within the disciplines of fiction must involve us in considerations of authorship and viewpoint. For that reason my next chapter will treat the two issues as one identifying film-making with direction and presenting the director's vision and skill as major sources of value in the cinema. The position assumed here will be argued later.

5 The World and Its Image

The crucial difference between 'the natural event and its appearance on the screen' is not physical but psychological. The film medium can never become 'too lifelike' to offer a valid fictional form so long as we retain our awareness of the distinction between film and reality; that is so long as we remain spectators rather than participants. Technology may yet develop the extent and fidelity of the movie's reproduction in many ways. But it cannot duplicate reality because it cannot directly reproduce our perception of reality. What we see in the world is so much more a product of our will and whim than what we see on the screen. Recording presupposes the selection of viewpoint and thereby restricts our normal freedom to survey the world, to pursue and investigate the objects that catch our attention. In the movies we have to accept the point of view given to us. Our activity in the cinema, discounting the extra-curricular enjoyments of courtship, arson and malicious damage, is very limited. We can watch. We can listen. All the rest is in the mind. We cannot cross the screen to investigate the film's world for ourselves. We are more or less impotent in relation to the image because it presents actions already achieved and recorded; it gives us no influence and allows no possibility of intervention or effective protest.

But since it is not possible to affect the course of events, it is not necessary either. If we are without power we are also without responsibility. Our exclusion from the world so vividly represented frees us from the need to consider what we see in terms of an active response. We can observe the progress of a fire with that much more attention when it can be neither our business to put it out nor our concern to escape. We concentrate on what we see the more closely because we are not obliged to sacrifice inspection to involvement or flight.

Seeing safely is, in part, seeing without being seen. We can stare at screen characters, invade their most private actions and reactions, with an openness and persistence which decency forbids us to extend to the couple in the next row. Involving no risk and no responsibility, the cinema becomes a privileged area within which inspection and reaction can be quite free and unembarrassed. Awareness of our submission to the given viewpoint guarantees the maintenance of a 'screen' between us and the world of pictures. The screen which limits us protects us as well. Our detachment, despite the intense scrutiny which it allows, has nothing to do with objectivity in the Bazin-Kracauer sense. The 'impartiality of the lens' cannot be transferred to our vision so as to eliminate preconceptions and subjectivity. While the camera may record a fact dispassionately, we as spectators can react to the fact with the same prejudice in the cinema as in reality. If we could rid ourselves of knowledge and our customary patterns of thought, we could not make sense of a movie. We need our preconceptions because the film-maker needs his conventions, to create structure and sense for a type of vision which is divorced from so much of the normal manner and purpose of perception. Without a body of conventions, developed and learned as a shared system, the film-maker could not exploit the flexibility of film to achieve freedom of manoeuvre in time and space. If he did so, we would be unable to reassemble the fragmented images and make them cohere as a portrait of a world.

The capabilities of any communications device are limited by the capabilities of the 'receptor mechanism'. The slow development of movie techniques in the first twenty years of the cinema's history demands more than a technological explanation. We must assume also that the basic conventions could only gradually be established and extended. Many of the film-maker's devices are so obvious, apparently natural, to the modern spectator that they demand no conscious act of interpretation. But, according to Balazs, 'when Griffith first showed a big close-up in a Hollywood cinema and a huge "severed" head smiled at the public for the first time, there was panic in the cinema'.[1]

However distrustful we may be of that account, we need not doubt that the movie's liberation from the constraints of the camera and the eye was a difficult process involving much trial and error on both sides of the screen. The process has often been presented as one of escape from the alien conventions of the theatre, but such a view may undervalue the theatrical as a point of reference enabling the movie to gain a foothold in the world of fiction. The narrative possibilities of a medium designed to represent reality on the move are obvious to us only because we have seen some of them realized. But the reproduction of an existing form of story-telling, with the film-goer given the customary view of the performance through the stage's 'missing wall', may have been an indispensable first step on the route towards independent forms. An evolution by means of increasingly rapid 'scene changes' then becomes comprehensible, because it would be a development with which the audience might be expected to keep pace. Similarly the mobility of the camera seems to have been tied, initially, to the presentation of mobile settings, like cars and railway carriages, whose static frames could stabilize the shifting background. Once the audience had become accustomed to these effects, the way was prepared for an independently mobile image which would not disconcert the spectator by presenting him with a world gone adrift. Though this is an area in urgent need of detailed research, there is much to indicate that new technical devices become useful in the story film only after the audience has been introduced to them in other contexts, notably that of reportage. There the guaranteed authenticity and the predictable, often known or narrated, course of events gives the spectator a stable base against which to gauge the distortions of the jump-cut in time or the zoom-shot in space so that he can re-establish the image in terms of reality.

Provided that we do not become ensnared in crude equations with speech or writing, there is much sense in treating the technical conventions as a form of language which guides the connections we make and allows us to re-establish a stable frame for the movie's

1. Balazs, *Theory of the Film*, p. 35.

dislocated scales of time and space. In the fiction film the stability which cannot be found in the image is assigned to the movie's 'world'. We are directed to assume that this world exists beyond and around the part of it that is presented at any given moment. Our eyes see the world only as it is shown; our minds are encouraged to see it much more solidly. When we are asked to give the fictional reality a more extensive existence than it has on the screen we are asked to suppose that the world and the events occurring within it exist independent of camera, film and screen. In effect, it is assumed that our major focus of interest will not be images, but objects, persons, actions and events. Provided that it is recognizable, an object presented on the screen remains first and foremost an object and only secondarily a visual pattern.

The primary appeal of the movies depends on what we see rather than on the way we see it. Film publicists, not generally the most perceptive beings, were quick to realize this fact. The advertising copy for Griffith's *Judith of Bethulia* (1914) ran, in part, as follows:

Most expensive Biograph ever produced. More than one thousand people and about three hundred horsemen. The following were built expressly for the production: a replica of the ancient city of Bethulia; the mammoth wall that surrounded Bethulia ... The following spectacular effects: the storming of the walls of Bethulia; the hand to hand conflicts; the death-defying chariot charges at break-neck speed ... And overshadowing all, the heroism of the beautiful Judith.

Film theory has every reason to follow the copy-writer's lead by transferring emphasis from what the camera and the film create to what they allow to be created. In doing so, it will recognize that the director's most significant area of control is over what happens *within* the image. His control over the action, in detail, organization and emphasis, enables him to produce a personal treatment of the script situation. On occasion the treatment can be so personal as to constitute a reversal of the attitudes contained in the script. There is a scene in *55 Days at Pekin* where Charlton Heston, an army commander, has to go to the Anglican mission to tell a motherless young half-Chinese girl that her American father has been killed in action. It seems probable, to the point of certainty, that the scene was conceived by its writers as an opportunity to milk a few easy tears. But the director, Nicholas Ray, rejects the invitation. His treatment takes the emphasis away from the pathos in the situation of the orphaned half-caste. Instead, it directs our attention to the difficulties experienced by Heston through his inability to deal with emotional commitments, responsibilities or demands. He does not behave like a man normally reticent in attempting to reduce the shock of bereavement. He makes no attempt to comfort the child. His behaviour conveys fear that his words may produce a reaction which he cannot control or give rise to demands which he cannot meet.

The emphasis is transferred in a number of ways. Firstly, through the use made of dialogue which is written along conventional lines: 'I have some bad news for you.' 'Is it my husband/wife/son/dog?... Is he hurt?... Is he... dead?' and so on. We've seen, heard and read this scene many, many times. But here it is presented with a difference. It becomes Heston's way of making the girl break the news to herself. She does not volunteer her questions. She asks them only when Heston's embarrassed silence forces her to do so. Each time, she waits for him to carry on from his mumbled reply. Each time, he remains silent, seeming to hope that she will be satisfied to guess the truth without further conversation.

Heston is careful to avoid the risk of physical contact. He places the girl at the end of a bench and sits, inaccessibly huddled, in the other corner. He seldom, and briefly, raises his eyes to meet her anxious stare. He takes up her rag doll and gazes at it, preferring to address such remarks as he must make towards an impassive object.

Ray's direction does not destroy the pathos of the scene. But his treatment of the physical and verbal action establishes a counterpoint of harsh irony which lifts the sequence clear of its threatened sentimentality. By concentrating on Heston rather than the young orphan, the director integrates what might easily have been a mere weep-break in the movie's action. The scene becomes a necessary expansion of the film's portrayal of the professional soldier as a man for whom the direct physical conflicts of war offer an escape from more subtle and demanding human relationships.

The director does not have to subvert the script in order to make a recognizably personal impact. Most often he sets out to intensify an effect implicit in the shape of the narrative. But his way of doing so shows us what, for him, are the important elements in the action. Vincente Minnelli's comedy *The Courtship of Eddie's Father* contains an early scene in which the child Eddie and his father are preparing lunch together. It is Eddie's first day back at school since his mother's death. Both father and son are making an effort to adjust to their new circumstances and to help each other by discussing their feelings openly. Eddie replies to an inquiry about his morning at school by saying that he didn't do much: there was something he wanted to do, but he didn't; he wanted to cry.

During this brief episode Eddie is perched on top of a kitchen stool, taking down a cup and saucer from the wall-cupboard. This action is in no way dictated by John Gay's script. It presents the director's view of that moment in the relationship between father and son. Firstly, it puts their shared bereavement in a very ordinary context: the day-to-day household routine of preparing the dinner table. At the same time it presents, in the most direct way, the empty strangeness of their situation: Eddie is doing something which, ordinarily, would have been left to mother. The action also takes us graphically inside Eddie's mind and feelings by stressing the instability of his emotional balance. Eddie's precarious physical position on the stool, his careful handling of two fragile objects, counterpoint his attempt at emotional poise.

This is clearly very skilful as a job of direction. The harshness of the action – cup and saucer rattle unpleasantly as, on 'I wanted to cry', Eddie brings them together – makes the episode solid and convincing so that it is both very moving and completely void of sentimentality. Also, the emphasis on Eddie's emotional frailty prepares us for a subsequent scene in which he will break down at the sight of a dead goldfish. But it is not skill alone which is exhibited here. The actions which the director has chosen present a personal viewpoint on the sequence. In particular, Minnelli's decision to put a highly-charged conversation into so ordinary a perspective embodies a specific attitude to the narrative.

It is the director's role as governor of the action which is most consistently neglected by the film theorists (and by many critics) who tend to see direction exclusively in terms of the camera and the cutting bench. This is understandable since the director cannot afford to make his contribution to the action at all obvious. What happens on the screen must not emerge as a directorial 'touch' detached from the dramatic situation; otherwise the spectator's belief in the action will decrease or disappear. The director's guiding hand is obvious only when it is too heavy.

Hitchcock's *Marnie* provides a fine instance of the way in which action can be moulded at the same time 'invisibly' and to precise effect. Twice, at moments of crisis, his heroine turns her face towards a wall and clings to it, as if trying to absorb herself into its fabric. At first sight this gesture seems to be *only*, what it undoubtedly is, an extremely skilful way of conveying to the spectator the full measure of Marnie's panic. But, more closely examined, the gesture takes us to the heart of her character and directs us to the film's central theme. We see that the action is a very childish one, closely analogous to hiding one's head in one's mother's skirt, and is related to a childish belief. The underlying assumption is that by making oneself blind one becomes invisible, that one cannot be harmed by something that one refuses to see. Marnie's greatest mistake – significantly linked with both her childhood and her desire for maternal protection – is the belief that reality is escapable. The destructive nature of such self-deceit is Hitchcock's main subject in this picture.

The creation of significant gesture here serves to show what I mean by the 'invisible' effect. The spectator can understand the action of the sequence without becoming aware of the device as relevant comment. It does not *demand* interpretation. But if he does examine the device and relate it to his knowledge of the heroine the significance of the moment is enhanced.

The director's control over what happens extends beyond the details of the performances to cover the 'behaviour' of objects. This too can be given expressive effect. In Nicholas Ray's *Johnny Guitar* a funeral party becomes a lynch mob when the mourners set out to capture the dead man's suspected killers. The victim's sister, Emma, rides with the posse. As she forces up the speed of the pursuit, the wind carries away her black-veiled hat to be trampled in the dust beneath galloping hooves. The 'action' of the hat amplifies our view of the character: grief for the loss of her brother is not the motive guiding Emma's actions, and her sorrow has been forgotten in the exhilaration of the chase.

Nothing in the story or dialogue obliged the director to include this action in the sequence. It was invented to convey a particular view of Emma's character and motives. But we can respond to it simply as information; within the film's world it happened because Emma was in such a hurry, not because it was significant.

In terms of action and image the direction prepared us for this moment in the film. Our first sight of Emma was when she rode on an earlier errand of persecution. She arrived outside the heroine's saloon during a dust storm, the wind driving behind her so that she had to clutch on to her hat. As she reined in her horse she seemed in danger of being carried away on the storm. The organization here impressed us with the feeling, confirmed and developed by her later actions, that Emma had almost lost control over the pressures that drove her.

The impression of dangerous instability was developed from the action by the image. Emma's arrival was observed by the heroine and by us, from an upstairs window. The solid stillness of its frame set off the turbulence and insecurity of her movements: Emma's difficulty in holding her ground was emphasized for us by the fact that if she failed to do so she would disappear from sight.

This shot is a beautiful example of the balance between action and image that skill can achieve. This balance, the delicate relationship between what is shown and the way of showing, justifies and exalts the movie's mongrel confusion of reportage with narrative and visual art. A single image is made to act both as a recording, to show us what happens, and as an expressive device to heighten the effect and significance of what we see.

But such balance will go unappreciated unless we respond to movies as a synthetic form, since none of the elements in the synthesis has a separate importance. The parts are of interest as we relate them, not in isolation. A literary approach, as adopted by most reviewers in the press and in allegedly specialized magazines, *reduces* the film narrative to a verbal statement and then tries to assess the value and significance of the resulting form of words. No distinction is drawn between the film story and its verbal synopsis. The example under discussion, stripped of all that it gains by its presentation in movie terms, amounts to nothing more interesting than this: 'Emma arrives on horseback during a dust-storm.'

At the other end of the scale the orthodox theorist, ignoring the film's 'reality' in his quest for the more blatant 'filmic' effects, will find no meaning in the image. It does not offer a visualized concept, nor does it contribute to an ostentatious editing pattern. The movement of 'spot and shape' is not abstract or quasi-symphonic. It is the movement of a real woman on a real horse. The image has been contrived to appear natural, almost unavoidable. It is significant only within its context of narrative and character development, just as the image of Emma's hat has expressive value only as the hat of a particular woman at a given point in a specific story.

A synthetic approach corrects the critic's literary bias towards portentous narrative and his purist bias towards visual bombast. In the process it centres our attention on the normal function of the director: not to devise stories and not to construct painterly patterns but to realize given material and organize it into significant form. In order to comprehend whole meanings, rather than those parts of the meaning which are present in verbal synopsis or visual code, attention must be paid to the whole content of shot, sequence and film. The extent to which a movie rewards this complete attention is an index of its achievement.

Consider this sequence from *Carmen Jones*, Otto Preminger's film version of Oscar Hammerstein's musical comedy version of Georges Bizet's opera version of Prosper Mérimée's (not very) original tale. The soldier hero, Joe, is driving a jeep down a country road. Beside him sits his prisoner Carmen, whom he has been ordered to deliver to the civilian authorities in a near-by town. As the jeep speeds along, Carmen makes a pass at Joe; she sings her invitation to abandon duty and run away to the shared excitements of her favourite night-spot.

The camera records the beginning of her song from the jeep's bonnet, seeing both the prisoner and her guard within the windscreen's stable frame. A metal strut at the centre of the windscreen divides the image so as to isolate and confine each character within a separate visual cage. But Carmen's movements shatter the rigid symmetry of the image. First she wriggles to Joe's side of the jeep, thrusting herself across the barrier into his cage. Then, her advances rejected, she transfers to the back seat to gain greater freedom of movement in a less restricted space. Preminger stresses the significance of her movement by changing the camera's viewpoint and making the image share in Carmen's liberation. The picture achieves a new openness now that the action is seen from alongside the jeep, with the frame of the windscreen no longer enclosing our view. The fresh angle conveys also a much stronger feeling of movement since it brings into play what the previous shot had suppressed, the rapid flow of the background scenery. Its fluid, varied pattern reinforces the free-ranging rhythms of Carmen's song.

Remarkable in this short sequence is the way that character, ideas and states of mind are projected visually without compromising the credibility of the image. The first shot begins as a graphic expression of Joe's personality. It shows us his world as he wishes to see it – a world of order and stability. But as the shot develops we see that the order is rigid and inhibiting, the stability unnatural, claustrophobic and rather lifeless.

Where Joe submits, Carmen challenges; the latter part of the shot gives us her view of Joe's world. She will not be contained within a static discipline. She rejects external restraints; demands licence to act according to her own needs and impulses. She makes a brief effort to assert her freedom within Joe's structured world, by exploding the neat symmetry of 'his' composition.

In the second shot she has given up the attempt. We are offered a picture of her world, and a direct contradiction of the previous image. This world is open, vigorous, fluid, but also chaotic and essentially aimless. There is plenty of movement but it exists for its own sake, to satisfy a restless craving, without direction. Preminger's camera extracts full value from the scenery's flashing passage, but we never see where the jeep is going. The framing of the picture cuts off our view so as to deny the suggestion of a goal.

The contrast between the two images summarizes the conflict between Carmen and Joe; but the development of the sequence, carrying us from Joe's world into Carmen's, conveys also Joe's mounting involvement.

All this, again, is a matter of direction. Not that the images are isolated, as the director's work, from plot and action: we can assign a specific significance to Preminger's treatment only because it brings out possibilities latent in the story and dialogue. The images have meaning in the first place because they are consistent with what we already know about Carmen and Joe. (They would lack sense if we were watching, say, a happy couple driving off on a country picnic.) But, given basic coherence, the direction extends our awareness of the characters and of the ways of life they represent.

In doing so it transforms what is, in synopsis, a rather familiar situation: brassy dame makes unsuccessful play for disapproving male. Hammerstein's lyric is admirable in many ways but it makes no claim to depth of insight. On disc (as a complete account of the sequence's verbal and musical material) 'There's a Café on the Corner' is pleasantly provocative but not much more. The scene as written contains no suggestion of the clash between modes of thinking and living which the film evokes, nor of Joe's changing attitude. These are conjured up in various ways by the translation from text to image.

The physical presences of the actors – in particular the abundant sensuality of Dorothy Dandridge's Carmen – and our preconception of the way the story will go, both play a large part in guiding our reactions. It is not in order to deny the impact of these elements that I assign first importance to Preminger's treatment. But if we examine the scene in terms of the options open to the director on the first day of filming we find that very little of the treatment was dictated by the scenario. It was necessary only that Carmen sing her invitation. Her actions and movements, Joe's reactions, the angle of vision and the structure of the images, the moment and method of cutting, all these details were freely chosen.

Yet it is precisely the shaping of these details that inflects the scene with its particular mood and meaning. Even the most fundamental decision, the one which preconditions all the others, was a matter not of plot but of treatment: there is nothing in the lyric or the story which obliges the director to place the scene in an open jeep on a country road. It is unlikely to have been staged this way in Hammerstein's version. On film it could be presented no less credibly at the army base before the journey begins, during a break in the journey (at, for example, a petrol station), or in an entirely different kind of transport. Any of these settings would have created a new range of possibilities for action and image. The selection of this setting with this treatment embodies a view of the characters at this moment in their story.

Throughout *Carmen Jones* the contrasts between open and closed images, static and mobile action, are worked out to give this version of the familiar story a specific and unexpected significance. Narrative, dialogue and music are assembled from a wide variety of sources; the meaning of Preminger's film has one dominant source – the direction. But what matters is less the originality or otherwise of Preminger's theme than the freshness, economy and intelligence of the means by which the theme is presented.

The same point emerges clearly if we examine an image from Richard Brooks's *Lord Jim*. The hero, a dreamer haunted by his vision of an inhuman grandeur, is standing on a fog-bound raft in the middle of a river. By his side is Gentleman Brown, the cynical chief of a gang of cut-throats. Brown is trying to persuade Jim to arrange his escape from an ambush; his remarks repeatedly hint at bonds, recognized or obscured, that make Jim 'one of us'. While they talk, Jim, fair-haired and dressed in light colours, faces out across the water, raising his right hand to lean against the raft's guide-rail. Then Brown, a swarthy, black-bearded figure in bowler hat and dark suit, takes up the same position – except that he holds to the rail with his left hand. The image is briefly shown, but it lasts long enough for us to appreciate the psychological implications of its structure: Brown is Jim's dark reflection, his unrecognized mirror-image, so much his opposite as to be almost a replica.

The director can scarcely be given credit for the thought that shapes this image. It is an aspect of the Jim-Brown relationship than Conrad suggests in the novel from which the film derives, and one which Conrad's commentators have explored at some length. Brooks invented not the idea but the image which expresses it in movie terms. The value we can claim for the image derives from its simultaneous credibility and significance. Image and meaning arise from believable action. The behaviour of Jim and Brown exist solidly in the film's world; the image is achieved without strain as the camera observes their movements.

By contrast, Joseph Losey's *The Criminal* contains a prison sequence in which one of the convicts talks, half to himself, of the ways in which men can try to combat the numbing effect of a long sentence. The camera moves in on him as he speaks, so that the greater part of his monologue is delivered in close-up. At the same time the lights behind him are dimmed until his face is seen isolated against a black background.

As a means to eliminate distraction, to centre complete attention on the prisoner's face and words, the device here is quite legitimate. But the actual effect contradicts that intention since it merely substitutes one distraction for another: we might have watched what other characters were doing in the depths of the corridor; we certainly stop to wonder what's happening to the current back there. The effort of adjusting to an incredible lighting scheme is not conducive to concentration. Light is less flexible, less readily subject to rapid alteration than composition, which evolves with every movement of object, character and camera. Within any given setting we expect the source of illumination – whether it is shown or deduced – to remain constant unless we are given an acceptable reason for a change. A character on the screen can turn lights on and off at will. The director behind the camera does not have the same freedom unless he is willing to draw attention to himself at the expense of the film's action. Since the effectiveness of the film depends on our being literal-minded in our response to the image there is nothing to be gained by the deliberate creation of discrepancies.

Within the framework of maintained belief, lighting, even more than composition, is dependent on action and setting. Designing an effect with light involves devising the means to make the effect credible.

Nicholas Ray's *Rebel Without a Cause* covers twenty-four hours in the life of a disturbed adolescent. At one point in the story the hero is challenged to a 'chicken run' by the leader of a delinquent gang. The chicken run is a trial of nerves in which the contestants drive two cars at top speed over the edge of a sheer cliff – the first to jump before reaching the edge being declared 'chicken'. The lighting in this sequence stresses the self-enclosed, artificial excitements of the game. The use of spot- and flood-lights helps to give the scene a feeling of theatre and draws attention to the deliberation with which the event is stage-managed, so that we see it as something very close to a tribal rite, at once gratuitous and intense.

The lighting effect is essential to the feeling and significance of the sequence, as a channelling of our response so that we see the events 'in the same light' as the director. But it is not, as in *The Criminal*, obviously controlled from behind the camera. The illumination is traced to a quite credible source: the headlamps of the cars which other gang members, spectators, have drawn up along the sides of the course.

Indeed, Ray is able to profit from the necessity of motivating his spotlights: the ritual nature of the action is emphasized by the manner in which, at the word of command, all the headlamps are directed on to the arena. To make the desirable look unavoidable, to take what is available and make it meaningful, that is a large part of the great director's secret.

We can see a similar intelligence at work, in relation to colour, in another of Ray's pictures – *Bigger than Life*. This one has a depressed middle-class setting. Its hero, a teacher with a heart ailment working to support his wife and young son, leaves school at the end of the day to start his evening job in the offices of a taxi company. As he walks away from the school building with its background of respectable greys and browns, the image dissolves into a general view of the cab-park photographed so that the screen is virtually covered with the garish yellow of the taxi-ranks.

The transition thus handled gains an emotional colouring which conveys not only the physical strain under which the man lives, but also his *déclassé* feeling of shame in his secondary occupation.

The colour here is 'natural'. It comes from an apparently objective recording of phenomena which we would expect to find in the settings presented: grey walls and dark brown doors on a school, bright yellow cabs in an (American) taxi pool. But it is just because we are not given reason to question the credibility of the colour that we can give the full emotional response that the arrangement of colour requires.

By contrast, the colour effects that film-reviewers most commonly single out for praise are precisely those which, by rejecting credibility, encourage a purely cerebral recognition. In Antonioni's *The Red Desert*, red is used to represent the threat which the neurotic heroine fears from an alienated, hostile and disintegrating world. Towards the end of the film she is made love to while on the verge of complete mental collapse. And from shot to shot the bedpost becomes an ever more threateningly glaring red. We observe that colour is being used to create an effect. Intellectually we can identify the effect required. But of the effect itself we feel no symptom. We are so busy *noticing* that we respond rather to our awareness of the device than to the state of mind it sets out to evoke.

Richard Brooks worked with the same sort of effect in his version of *The Brothers Karamazov*. But he profited from his experience and in a subsequent film, *Elmer Gantry*, produced something close to a classic example of colour moulded throughout a scene without ruptures in continuity of décor or lighting. Elmer, a hard-drinking and promiscuous hardware salesman, has fallen in love with the evangelist Sister Sharon and joined her mission as a rabble-rousing hot-gospeller. He comes to her bedroom one morning to propose a pleasure trip away from the clamorous demands of the salvation-seekers. The mood of gay irresponsibility is reflected and enhanced by the light colours that predominate: the walls of the bedroom bathed in early morning sunshine, the soft colours of the bedclothes and Sharon's nightgown, Elmer's white sailing cap and (in this light) cheery blue blazer.

Elmer goes to answer a knock on the door of the bedroom's

antechamber. Here the walls are dark green, but the light from the bedroom keeps the colours cheerful enough, especially when the image is brightened by the pleasant pale tones of Sharon's dressing-gown as she hurries out to meet the visitor. Elmer opens the door to Bill, Sharon's business manager; his dark, elderly suit brings another gloomy colour into the picture. He says that he wants to speak to Elmer alone. Sharon goes into her bedroom to change, removing from the scene its principal light colour.

When the bedroom door is closed the sunlight is blocked so that both Elmer's navy jacket and the green walls take on an unpleasantly darker aspect. Moreover the door itself gives the image a central mass of murky brown. Bill produces a series of compromising photographs featuring Elmer and his vengeful ex-mistress; the mission is being blackmailed; Sharon will have to be told. The sombreness of the scene is completed by the re-entry of Sharon, now in a dark grey dress.

As evidence of colour thinking this is quite a formidable scene in the way that its modulations of tone chart the gradual stages of a descent from one mood to its opposite. But it is even more remarkable for the fact that at no time can its manipulation of colour disturb the most literal-minded spectator. Although its fluidity doubtless masks several hours of solid work from the cameraman and designers, there is no point at which lighting or décor undergo changes that are not directly and credibly motivated by the movements of the actors. Nor is there a point at which any of the actors is seen to move, without credible purpose, simply in order to bring about a change in colour values.

In his use of the camera the director is freed from the discipline of credibility. The position or movement of the camera, however extraordinary, need not affect our belief in the film as record, unless the event itself is falsified – as it is in *The Criminal* and *The Red Desert* – simply in order to create an image. In both these cases the director's effort to point the *meaning* of an action blunts the raw impact of the action itself. The process is self-defeating since it calls attention to the director at the expense of the events *through* which he set out to convey meaning.

Striving for a camera style which is effective and significant but not distracting, the director escapes the discipline of credibility to discover those of clarity and economy. An early sequence in John Frankenheimer's *The Train* shows the German forces preparing to withdraw from their occupation of Paris. The camera's convulsive movements emphasize the urgent confusion in the army headquarters as its staff rush about seeing to the storage or destruction of military documents.

There is no doubt that Frankenheimer's treatment is capable of conveying the required effect; the sequence can indeed impress upon us its atmosphere of crisis and chaos. Yet we can observe also a disproportion between the effect produced and the means employed to produce it. In terms of atmosphere the scene is successful; it remains very questionable on the level of style since it so strongly recalls the old sayings about mountains and mice, sledgehammers and nuts. The disparity between end and means is felt because the camera movements are superimposed on the action. They do not seem to spring from a view of the events portrayed. Given that the camera is to be used to heighten the atmosphere of panic, there still seems to be no reason in this sequence to move it in one direction rather than any of a dozen others.

Compare and contrast the following shot, from Preminger's *The Cardinal*. Stephen Fermoyle has been granted a year's leave of absence from the priesthood and has taken a teaching post in Vienna. During the summer vacation he is shown the scenic and architectural beauties of Austria by Anne-Marie, a gay and flirtatious young woman who is unaware of his profession. The sequence opens with the two of them cycling down a hillside in the country. The camera turns to follow their descent as they glide round a bend in the road, its movement embracing a wide, sinking arc until it comes to rest on the huge open landscape spread out before them. The movement, amplified by the composer's expansive waltz theme, conveys to us the exhilaration and release that Fermoyle discovers in his relationship with the girl, his sense of new and attractive possibilities opening up for him.

Here Preminger is using for its emotional effect the transition from an enclosed to an open image and the physical impact of camera movement projected on to the large cinema screen. The image conveys a feeling of exhilaration and release which we transfer into the dramatic situation. The director is thus able to make us aware of Fermoyle's emotions without filming a dialogue on the subject or – later – a love scene. On the other hand, the shot exists in the context of the story as a simple and uncluttered record of the way in which the young couple spend their time together. Its beauty, in film terms, derives from its concentration: a single shot is made to carry both the exposition and the meaning; fact and feeling are communicated in one necessary image. The shot is effective precisely because the camera is used here as a 'mere recording instrument'. Preminger's image does not cease to offer information in order to impose a mood or meaning. Instead the viewpoint is used to provoke, out of all the possible responses to the action, the ones most relevant to the film's design. Neither the event nor any aspect of the presentation has value in an arbitrary, theoretical isolation. The value comes from a complex circuit of reactions; meanings are generated from the give-and-take-and-give-again with which event and viewpoint interact.

In Hitchcock's *Rope*, for example, camera movements are employed to deepen our knowledge of each of the main characters. But their effectiveness is inseparable from the actions they present; they prompt us to notice things about the characters, not the camera, or rather to notice the image primarily in terms of the action. The film's two heroes, Brandon and Philip, murder a young man for the thrill of committing the perfect, motiveless crime. His corpse is to be concealed in Brandon's apartment during a dinner party at which they will entertain members of the victim's family, his fiancée and two of his friends. Early in the film Brandon, the dominant partner in the scheme, walks from sitting-room to kitchen carrying the murder weapon, a length of rope. The camera follows him at a distance and directs our attention to the exhilarated arrogance of his walk. It stops at the kitchen door, but Brandon walks through and in the brief moment of the swing-door's rebound we see him drop the rope into a drawer. Here the flashy precision of the camera effect informs our view of Brandon; the split-second control of the image becomes a projection of Brandon's evil assurance and calculation.

This tiny episode from Hitchcock's picture summarizes the to-and-fro of doing and showing that comes under the director's control. While highlighting a particular quality of gesture and movement, the motion of the camera itself takes on that quality. As it follows Brandon, its own movement becomes menacingly arrogant. It works like this because the image amplifies and redefines expectations created by Brandon's actions, words and manner, not because the movement of the camera has any quality that can be distinguished from the events with which it keeps pace.

In the same sequence a very similar movement produces an opposite effect. The image absorbs and reflects the terrified submissiveness of Brandon's accomplice, Philip, in the way that the camera follows after him as he trails through the flat in Brandon's wake. Towards the end of the film its short, halting movements become ever more closely identified with Rupert, Brandon's suspicious friend. His dread of what his investigations may produce is pictured in its tentative and fearful probings.

These stunted camera movements are a product of Rupert's hesitant manoeuvres. But Rupert's actions are in turn conditioned by the setting: in the last part of *Rope* the camera and the action are confined within a single room whose furnishings hinder mobility. The restriction of space, climaxed here, has been taking place since the film began. The whole action is contained within Brandon's flat, but at the opening of the picture movement is relatively free. Actors and camera pass back and forth several times through the sitting-room, hallway and dining-room. Later the action is limited to the sitting-room and hallway. But from the moment when Rupert returns to confirm his suspicions it is restricted to the sitting-room alone.

The claustrophobia which Hitchcock creates by closing in the décor is an essential part of our experience of the film. It mounts continuously until the point where Rupert, having discovered the corpse, opens a window to summon the police by firing a revolver into the night air. We have entered the apartment to witness the commission of a crime. Gradually we become aware that we shall be shut in until the crime is exposed. By the relentless increase of our confinement Hitchcock makes us feel that the exposure is as necessary as it is inexorable. Necessary not so much in relation to the murderers – on the simple level of crime and punishment – but rather for Rupert. The film shows him forced to live through and recognize the real implications of his professed beliefs. It carries him, and us, towards the realization that intellectual assent to a particular idea – in this case, fascist – must involve moral complicity in its actual operation.

The mounting claustrophobia communicated by Hitchcock's treatment demonstrates again how a director can make artistic virtue out of a plot requirement. *Rope* is adapted from a stage play whose action is confined to one set. The confinement is essential to its story and Arthur Laurents's screenplay, while it makes many other changes, respects the structure of the piece. A considerable degree of visual restriction is therefore inherent in the film project. Where another director might attempt to counteract the theatrical enclosure of the action, in the supposed interest of Cinema, Hitchcock exploits it. He shapes it as a vital development of his theme by employing a décor which allows progressive limitation of the playing space.

Here, as in the jeep sequence from *Carmen Jones*, the film-maker uses a setting for its direct effect upon the shapes of action and image. But, in *The Courtship of Eddie's Father*, we have seen how a location also provides associations of its own to colour our view of events. Setting his scene in the kitchen, traditional domain of wife and mother, Minnelli gave the action a nuance that in school, street or living-room it would have lacked.

Perhaps we can best extend our consideration of the associative power of décor by looking at three different ways in which one director, Nicholas Ray, has used the particular concept of 'upstairs'. In *Johnny Guitar* upstairs represents isolation. The heroine Vienna, a saloon owner, attempts a rigid separation of public from private life; the former is lived on the ground floor of her establishment amid the drinks and the gaming tables, the latter in her upstairs retreat with its more delicate and feminine décor. Vienna is quite explicit about the distinction. Standing half-way down the stairs, gun in hand, she wards off the posse which has come to search her place: 'Down there I sell whisky and cards. All you can get up these stairs is a bullet in the head.' Throughout the film Ray modulates his images of action 'off the ground' and 'down to earth'. The conflict of settings becomes a thematic conflict: Vienna's isolationism versus the intrusions of a corrupt and demanding society.

In *Bigger than Life* upstairs suggests both the possibility of a normal family life and the temporary retreat from responsibilities into a dreamland. In Ray's own words, 'the upstairs were the areas of possible refuge, serenity and joy'. Travel posters decorating the walls become more exotic as they progress from Grand Canyon, by the front door, to Bologna, on the top landing. Upstairs represents the aspiration of the middle-aged, poorly paid schoolmaster to 'get away sometime'.

Rebel Without a Cause uses upstairs to point the failure of a man through his weakness as both husband and father. His son is shocked and hurt to find him, aproned, outside his bedroom and on his knees. He is timidly mopping up the mess he has made by dropping the supper tray he was bringing to his wife. The location of the sequence reinforces the performances to make us appreciate the young man's anger and anguish.

Ray's varied uses of the same basic location are effective largely because the setting and its connotations are common property. The spectator does not have to strain to make the required connections; his day-to-day experience provides the necessary background. In the Western Hemisphere at least, upstairs carries automatically the suggestions of privacy, rest, fantasy and male dominance which Ray employs.

By contrast, in *The Best Man* Franklin Shaffner has a scene where two contestants for their party's Presidential nomination meet privately in order to blackmail one another. To ensure secrecy they meet in the depths of the hotel which has been taken over for the convention – in an underground air-raid shelter. They are surrounded by huge canisters containing provision stored in case of nuclear attack.

Set down like this the intention is clear: a satiric counterpoint between the squalid machinations required of a Presidential candidate and the momentous importance of the President's office. However, the effect sounds better in words than it looks on the screen. Few of us have first-hand information about the appearance of a nuclear shelter. Before we can respond to the setting we have to identify it by reading the labels on the canisters. That we do this at all presupposes a certain relaxation of interest in the action of the scene, a transfer of effort from comprehension of the drama to interpretation of the décor. The point to consider, then, is not whether such a device is allowable (there is no question of that since the credibility of the film's world is in no way threatened) but how richly the décor's claim to attention is rewarded. We are surely well aware that our survival is largely by courtesy of the President of the USA. The irony which Shaffner strains to establish through the counterpoint of action and setting is therefore fully present in the story. There is a difference, unacknowledged here, between development and repetition.

The weakness of Shaffner's approach is suggested by the extent to which the use of décor can be separated from the other elements in the film's treatment. The particular setting is not part of a developing structure. It has been tacked on to the film, and for the purposes of discussion it can quite easily be unpinned. Little or nothing is lost in the passage from picture to prose. But the subtler organizations seldom admit of complete analysis; their power derives from a complex interaction of elements whose discussion as isolated *parts* of the treatment must result in falsifying the whole.

It is easy enough, for example, to indicate the function of the décor in the final sequences of Otto Preminger's *River of No Return*. In a one-street Western town the hardware store and the 'Black Nugget' saloon correspond to the ways of life, respectively, of the farmer hero (Robert Mitchum) and the 'chantoose' heroine (Marilyn Monroe). Their conflict is suggested by the positions of the two buildings on opposite sides of the street. But the possibility in the first place, and ultimately the achievement of a compromise is conveyed by the presence of the open road – spatially and symbolically a middle term between the two locales.

Such a crude statement of the décor's meaning courts ridicule, because in itself the décor has no meaning. The topography is not at all remarkable. It could quite well have been designed without expressive intent. And clearly if the store and saloon face one another there is going to be an open space between.

Still, the décor does bear the significance I have assigned, when we see it in its full context, the movie's development of action, character and theme. The saloon and the hardware store take on expressive relevance, become more than just *places*, because the film's story has been moulded to this point as a confrontation between two ways of thinking and living. Matt the farmer and the showgirl Kay have come to represent moral extremes, the one static and unbending, the other lacking purpose and definition; the one joyless, the other irresponsible. A too complete reliance on law and reason confronts an excessive surrender to intuition and feeling.

During a period of enforced cooperation both characters are made to face the unsatisfactory elements in their values; each is prompted to a certain sympathy with the other's point of view; and each makes a tentative move towards compromise. But at the end of this period, on arrival in the town, there is a reversion to the status quo. Matt and Kay return to the environments in which we first met them. Matt is seen against the background of tools and provisions needed to support the rigorous but productive life of an isolated farmstead. Kay crosses the street away from him to re-enter the easy but chaotic milieu of the saloons. The completeness of her re-absorption is signified by her exchanging the jeans and leather jacket which she wore on the journey with Matt for the loud, pseudo-erotic costume of a bar-room entertainer.

The 'middle-ground' significance of the open space is an extension of the relationship between character and décor. It is Kay, flexible and tolerant but unstable, who wanders back and forth across the road. Matt keeps firmly to his own side of the street. The camera emphasizes action across and within the middle ground. Its movements direct attention both to the distance dividing the store from the saloon and to the freedom with which this space may be used or crossed. The treatment conveys the possibility of choosing a position at or between the two extremes.

Initially, then, the décor derives its meaning from character and action. But once its relationship to them has been established, it begins to make its own contribution to the film. It gives the value of a deliberate concession to Matt's final gesture, when he crosses into Kay's territory to fetch her from the saloon. It gives the force of agreed compromise to the moment when, driving away with Matt along the open road, Kay throws off her gaudy red shoes. With action, décor and image in coherent relationship, space itself becomes charged with meaning.

The director's use of décor, in its possibilities and limitations, conforms to the pattern that has emerged from other aspects of our inquiry. Direction does not involve total freedom to locate actions or to design settings. Quite often a location is dictated by the plot and design controlled by the location. The director has to start from what is known or necessary or likely or, at the very least, possible. From this base he can go on to organize the relationship between action, image and décor, to create meaning through pattern. But credibility remains the controlling factor. The primary function of décor is to provide a believable environment for the action. Thereafter – but only thereafter – the director is free to work in, and on, the setting so as to develop the implications of its relationship to the action.

Similarly, we can say that the primary function of the image is to let us see the action. If the image is clear, it may also be meaningful. The significance of the treatment, and its artistic integrity, is conditional upon its credibility.

And so it is with sound. The primary function of the sound-track is to let us hear, to fill out the illusion by recording for our ears just as the image records for our eyes. The sound-track is sufficiently justified when it tells us what the characters are saying and how they say it. The demand, on allegedly artistic grounds, for 'a more cinematic use of sound' is most often a request for the introduction of noise divorced from its source, a decorative addition to the narrative rather than an organization of its elements: mixture as against synthesis. Decoration of this kind serves forcibly to remind us that the director is in control of the movie. It may also result in a less controlled film.

But, given that the director finds his effects *within* the action, the sound-track is more malleable than the image. Our ears are a great deal more selective and less critical than our eyes. We are continually surrounded by 'unheard' noises and there are few of us whose ears could guarantee to distinguish rain on a window from rice deftly poured into a metal box. Thus the director is not obliged to let us hear everything that comes within range of the microphone, as he is obliged to show all that falls within the camera's view. And he can afford within reasonable limits to doctor the quality as well as the quantity of sound. The image will underwrite our belief in the sound. We do not question that the noise in *Eddie's Father* is the rattling of *that* cup against *that* saucer. Again we are dealing with interaction: the image encourages us to accept the reality of the sound; the sound alerts our perception to particular aspects of the image.

With its greater selectivity the sound-track offers the director a heightening of the sounds that he does use, which in turn gives special opportunities for organization in terms of comparison and contrast. The theme of Roman Polanski's *Repulsion*, with its story of a young woman's descent into madness through sexual derangement, is crystallized in the likeness of the gasps of pleasure that the heroine's sister emits during copulation to the gasps of horror that convulse the same woman when she discovers a flayed corpse in her living-room.

In *The Cardinal* Preminger uses a contrast of sounds to create a remarkably ambiguous effect. The ambitious young priest has been sent, as a lesson in humility, to serve as assistant to the incumbent of a poverty-stricken parish in a remote corner of Massachusetts. As his train draws into the station the tinkling of its little bell refers us back to the grandeur of Rome with whose loud and heavy peals the film began. Thus the sound offers an ironic comment on Fermoyle's progress by emphasizing the isolation of this small community from the object of his ambitions. But it also links the two places so as to remind us that Stonebury,

Mass., is as much a part of the Church as the Vatican is: Fermoyle
is still on the road to Rome.

We may adapt our conclusion about lighting and say that with
sound also to design an effect involves devising the means to
make it credible by locating it within the film's world.

The death of the terrorist leader Akiva marks a vital stage in
the thematic development of *Exodus*. Preminger's treatment of the
scene relates the event to the policies which Akiva has advocated
and the values he has come to represent. The sound-track is one
of the means through which this relationship is conveyed.

Akiva's reserves of hatred and violence have found an outlet
in attacks upon the British in Palestine. He has just escaped from
prison and crashed through a road-block. And he is dying of
wounds received from British gunfire. While he dies the most
British of all melodies – 'Greensleeves' – breaks across the quiet
of the scene.

Here again a simplified description of a film effect shows only
what it *might* have been, a cheap irony blatantly superimposed on
the action by a bombastic director. For at least two reasons, the
effect does not work in this primitive way. The most important is
that the music is credibly presented. It comes from the car radio
which Akiva has switched on in order to follow the news reports
on his jail-break. Thus integrated into the action, the music acts
not as an obtrusive comment on the scene but as part of its
ordinary background – an observable 'fact' like the flowering
shrubs which surround Akiva's car.

A second reason is that the melody is heard not in Vaughan
William's pastoral setting – which again would have made the
music unconvincing and the irony of its Englishness too direct –
but in a lightly swinging sub-jazz arrangement. We can accept
this kind of music with its vacant jollity as a likely time-filler on a
services broadcasting network.

As a background effect, this music provokes a variety of
responses. The associations of the melody with all that is most
'British' offer an answer to Akiva and what he represents by
suggesting the futility of policies based on violence and hatred.
This has a particular importance in that Akiva has consistently

presented himself as a coldly efficient and rational strategist. At the same time the music partially endorses Akiva's indifference to the individual human life: the struggle for Israel is more important than the happiness or survival of any one Jew. In its speed and drive the music helps to maintain the atmosphere of crisis; and the fact that it comes from the radio keeps us in mind of the larger conflict surrounding this particular scene so that we feel a certain impatience with Akiva. There is simply not time to stand around in respect for an old man's dying moments.

The cheerfulness of the music further complicates our response. By contradicting our expectation of pathos it destroys any tendency towards complacent emotionalism. At the same time it reinforces a suggestion contained in David Opatoshu's performance – that this really is Akiva's 'happy ending' and that in all his actions the peace of death has been the ultimate though unrecognized goal.

This variety of conflicting reactions is possible because the music is kept in the background. There it can work by suggestion, to colour our response to the action. More assertively used, it would have captured the event by imposing a single statement of meaning and suppressing all but one of the possible interactions within the scene.

It is Preminger's skill here, as it is Minnelli's and Polanski's in the examples quoted, to annul the distinction between significant organization and objective recording. In this process the maintenance of credibility acts as a necessary discipline. The sound-track retains its primary function as a recording, but the recording is organized to serve other purposes as well. Of course, this is not the only way in which film-makers use sound; in other contexts such reticence might be a vice; but it is a method which can reconcile the cinema's divergent tendencies towards illusion and reality by matching the film-maker's personal vision against the camera's impersonal stare.

The composition of sound-tracks or images is a facility available to the director as an extension of their basic functions – to let us hear, to let us see. But it is a facility and not an obligation. In many of the finest films images and sounds are simply the means of presenting the essentials of the action as clearly as can be. The picture exists solely for what it shows and we gain nothing by attempting to interpret its structure. Its qualities as an image are submerged in its function as a document. Much film comedy, for example, operates along these lines. The camera is a privileged spectator as it records, say, the desperate gallantry with which Mr Grant wields his top hat to shield Miss Hepburn's unwittingly exposed and obstinately mobile rear. Why, in such a case, should it bother itself with questions of line and texture? The purely 'filmic' criteria fade into irrelevance. That is why the great comedies, with their insistence on action and their indifference to cinematic elaboration, have proved so difficult to assess within the terms proposed by traditional film theory.

The cinema's facilities are chiefly important for the opportunities they create, not for their 'demands'. This applies to the possibilities of editing as much as to any other of the director's resources: like the camera and the microphone it is important in the first place for what it *allows*. It gives the film-maker freedom to select what he will show of any given action; and that means freedom to decide *how* he will show it. Because he can cut, the director is given a chance of obtaining his ideal performance; he can work and re-work any moment in the action until it gives exactly what he wants; he can throw out anything that would spoil his design.

The edited film has a freedom that the camera's bulky eye cannot attain. The camera shares the physical limitations of its users; but once edited, the film is given the wild liberty of a mental process – of thought, imagination and dream.

Cutting shatters the real continuity of time and space to provide a major extension of the film's mobility. The whole notion of the 'shot', the possibility of recording any chosen fragment of an event from any chosen position, depends on the ability to re-assemble the fragments on the cutting bench and in the spectator's imagination. That is the primary, practical function of film editing – and its aesthetic justification. The means of getting from shot to shot is also one method, among many others, by which the film-maker may control pace and may give variety and shape to his images.

But with cutting, as with the other devices we have considered, the practical, informative function can be absorbed in a creative organization. From being merely useful, or permissive, editing becomes an essential part of the total style and meaning. Consider again the jeep ride from *Carmen Jones*. From one point of view we may see Preminger's cutting as a simple device which takes us from one viewpoint (front of jeep) to the other (alongside) while avoiding a difficult camera movement. The practical function of the editing, then, is simply to allow the director to present his two images – of Joe's world and of Carmen's. But the cut does more than that. By placing the two images in abrupt succession it creates a contrast that amplifies the significance of each of them: Joe's order is replaced by Carmen's freedom; the rigid stability of his image is contradicted by the restless fluidity of hers. The two distinct meanings are reinforced by so immediate a contrast. In theory a camera movement could have linked the two images. But that movement would have shown us Joe's world evolving into Carmen's: in other contexts a useful device, but here a contradiction of the story's clash between incompatible temperaments and conflicting ways of life. The camera movement would have given us Joe's world becoming Carmen's. The cut presents Carmen's world in opposition to Joe's.

The point here is not that either method must be approved or condemned. It is rather that each method carries its own connotations and its peculiar emphases, and that the meaning of a film sequence is controlled by such apparently insignificant details of presentation. Here the cut is 'better' than the camera movement because it relates more usefully to other aspects of the two images. In *Marnie*, Hitchcock's tormented heroine turns to her husband at a moment of psychological crisis to sob out her plea for salvation: 'O God, somebody help me!' The image fades on this line and takes us to a general view of the hallway as guests arrive for a party at which Marnie is to be presented to her husband's friends. The camera glides slowly towards the front door, stopping there to present in close-up the arrival of Strutt –

the businessman from whom Marnie has stolen several thousand dollars. The two shots are so constructed and linked that the second answers the first: Strutt is the somebody who comes in response to Marnie's plea.

From one point of view the editing is cruelly ironic in linking Marnie's cry for help with the arrival of the very character who can do most to destroy her comfort. Our involvement with Marnie is such that the irony has a very direct force.

But our attitude to the film's heroine is complex. We know a great deal about her which she refuses to recognize. We are increasingly aware of the gap between what she wants and what she needs. Strutt's arrival at this point conforms to the movie's major pattern: Marnie is obstructed by all that she most eagerly seeks; she is helped only by being forced to confront what she most desperately avoids. Linked with this pattern is another whereby a past whose memory Marnie has suppressed erupts menacingly into the present. While it is not the response that she – or we – looked for, Strutt's appearance *is* an answer to Marnie's cry. He is a part of the past which Marnie has to recognize before her agony can end.

The irony conveyed by Hitchcock's editing is an expression of the irony that the director finds in Marnie's whole situation. The tension that Hitchcock evokes by linking the two images embodies the film's essential conflict: identification with Marnie and her desires opposes knowledge of her most vital needs.

Richard Brooks's editing at the climax of *Elmer Gantry* uses different means to provoke a similar conflict. The evangelist Sister Sharon has graduated from tent-show revival meetings to ownership of a permanent 'temple' whose décor – part church and part music-hall – reflects the oddness of Sharon's vocation, its weird blend of religion and show-business. On the new tabernacle's opening night, Sharon is asked to heal a deaf man. She places her hands over his ears and the audience joins her in urgent prayer.

To this point the sequence has been constructed along Hitchcockian lines; its suspense principle is very similar to that of *Marnie*. On the one hand we want Sharon to get what she wants.

Curing the man's deafness would be the culmination of her success story – not only a full house on her opening night but a miracle as well! In addition the man's suffering is so clear and so touching that we want the miracle for his sake.

But here, as in *Marnie,* our involvement is incomplete. We respond to Sharon as a beautiful, perceptive, wry and vulnerable woman. But we are also fearfully aware of the delicate balance between Sharon's humanity and her ferocious dedication to her mission. We see how easily she could be tipped over the edge into religious megalomania.

Sharon's only prospect of happiness and sanity depends on her relationship with the reprobate Elmer. To this point it has remained possible that Elmer's charm and magnetism will prove strong enough to overcome the fierce pride of Sharon's belief in her vocation. She could choose obscurity with Elmer in preference to fame as the star attraction in a religious freak-show. The choice will be lost once she has achieved her miracle. She will have received too attractive a proof of her vocation. Beyond this there opens up a prospect of intolerable pressure on Sharon. She will be faced with demands for help not only from the lonely, confused and unhappy, but also from the crippled and the sick.

We are thus aware that the likely consequence of the miracle is disaster. But there is still a danger that our reasoned fears may be subdued by the scene's emotional force. The editing prevents this by its early introduction of a third strand in the narrative. As Sharon begins to pray, Brooks cuts away to show us a back-stage workman throwing down a cigarette stub. And amid the straining, shouting and praying by which Sharon achieves her miracle, we are constantly brought back to the draughty corner where the cigarette scorches and burns into a pile of paint-rags. By the time Sharon's patient declares himself healed our interest has been transferred to the impending catastrophe. Brooks's editing nullifies the emotional impact of the miracle by placing it in a dwarfing perspective.

It is enough that the organization breaks the mood of complacent yearning that the scene might easily have provoked. But it does more than that. Each time we cut back to see the steady kindling of the fire, it is as if the ash is being urged into flame by the very passions that Sharon ignites. The sequence carries the suggestion that the fire comes as a punishment for Sharon's presumption. It is in this scene that we are made to recognize the extent of the egoism underlying Sharon's quite genuine humility. She wants to serve her god. But she wants to be its chief servant. Brooks's cutting here complicates the film's predominantly agnostic tone. The healing miracle seems to assert a destructive threat; and the fire takes on the supernatural aspect of an Old Testament chastisement.

Those trained to recognize as creative montage only the more violently asserted conjunctions of stock-markets and battlefields, or palaces and slums, may well challenge my treating such a sequence as an example of significant editing. The director is *obliged* to show both the healing and the fire. After all, the fire 'does' break out during Sharon's performance. The cutting might seem to do little more than fulfil the demands of the story.

Yet if this were not so I could hardly quote the sequence as an example either of the director's craft or of the power over style and meaning that editing puts into his hands. If the sequence of shots were not to some extent inherent in the situation, Brooks's cutting would be arbitrary. Since most film-makers take pains to disguise the joins between shots, the argument for editing as a bearer of significance normally available to the director depends upon the claim that cutting can be effective and meaningful even when concealed; that is, when it seems to be a product of dramatic necessity rather than of the director's will, of the need to inform rather than the desire to comment.

In the matter of the director's authorship and creativity, that is surely the one point at issue. None will deny the responsibility of the director for effects (whether of editing, design or performance) which proclaim their aspiration towards meaning by their obtrusive irrelevance to the narrative. Suppose that the cuts away from Sharon's prayers had been, not back-stage, but to a forest fire. The symbolic relationship with the other elements in the sequence would have been thinner. But the symbolizing effort – embodiment of the destructive potential of mass hysteria – would have been more apparent. We would clearly be witnessing an 'editing effect'. By integrating the fire image into the action of the sequence, Brooks extends and complicates, at the same time as he 'conceals', its significance. The scenarist may have shaped the narrative so that the fire begins during Sharon's miracle-working. To have so placed the incendiary images that they assume relevance to the actions of Sharon and her audience is an achievement of direction.

The effect of the sequence derives less from a juxtaposition of *images*, as orthodox theory would dictate, than from an organization of events which editing in this case facilitates. The cruder effect of the forest fire would fit more readily into theories which present the cutting process as the crucial moment for artistic selection and for the creation of meaning.

The examples which can be quoted to uphold such a view of the cinema, those sequences where editing does function as the unique source of significance, are isolated and unrepresentative – even of the films from which they derive. One favourite example is drawn from Eisenstein's *Battleship Potemkin*. Just after the massacre on the Odessa Steps, the mutinied sailors turn the Potemkin's guns against the town's military headquarters. Images of destruction are followed by three shots of stone lions so photographed that we seem to see a single sleeping lion awaken and sit up in an attitude of surprise or alarm or anger or watchfulness.

It is certainly true that the images of the lions, taken separately, were without relevant meaning; hence that any significance that could be claimed for them arose from their juxtaposition. But that would demonstrate nothing more than that editing *may* assert meaning by imposing a relationship between disconnected objects and events. It does not show that editing is the sole means by which the elements of a film may be significantly related. Even less does it suggest that there is great merit in inserting dead matter into a movie in order to edit it into animation, subject it to the Life of a Thousand Cuts.

Rather, it seems a serious criticism of Eisenstein's device that the lions served no purpose in the movie beyond that of becoming components of a montage effect. They were not represented as, for example, elements of the Odessa setting, nor as targets for the *Potemkin*'s attack. The absence of connection, in terms of story, action, location – the absence of any dramatic connection at all – entailed an extreme imprecision of effect. The director's own interpretation was this: 'In the thunder of the *Potemkin*'s guns, a marble lion leaps up, in protest against the bloodshed on the Odessa steps.'[2] But that hardly fits the case.

If we interpret the image in context, the lion has dozed contentedly throughout the massacre. It sits up and takes notice only after the *Potemkin* has begun to retaliate. It would therefore seem more reasonable to think of it as awakened (and none too pleased about it) by the din of the guns; thus, to associate it with the military against the sailors and citizens – especially since it in no sense belongs to the battleship but could be connected with the other statuary we have seen, that decorating the general's HQ. That my insistence on the vagueness of the image is not simple perversity, Ivor Montagu demonstrates when he holds up for our admiration Eisenstein's 'single lion roused to fury by the thunder of a salvo from the rebel warship'.[3] As a symbol of authority the image could represent its anger, alarm, or even invincibility, since amid the destruction the statue itself suffers no damage. The case for Eisenstein's imagery here is not strengthened when we realize that its primary source is a Russian colloquialism meaning 'the very stones roared': roughly, 'all hell broke loose'. That merely underlines the literary nature of the effect. The problem is not that the symbol carries such a wide range of potential meanings, but that so little exists by which we can define its significance. Each reading seems as good or as weak as any other. The various interpretations are mutually exclusive, not mutually enriching.

But that must always be likely when a film-maker goes outside the dramatic components of a scene in order to find his imagery, or when he uses images whose connection with the surrounding objects and actions is purely visual – a matter of shape, colour,

2. Eisenstein, *The Film Form*, p. 56.
3. Ivor Montagu, *Film World – A Guide to Cinema*, Penguin Books, 1964, p. 117.

movement or rhythm alone. Our choice of meanings becomes arbitrary. So, equally, does the director's choice of image. Once 'outside' the scene, there seems little to choose between a stone lion and a real one, or between a lion of any sort and crashing waves, lightning storms, threshing machines and so forth.

Similarly with the hypothetical forest fire that I have foisted upon *Elmer Gantry*. In place of concrete detail – the paint-rags bundled back-stage suggesting the rushed completion of the temple, the workman who carelessly discards his cigarette *because* he's becoming preoccupied with events on-stage – Brooks could have sent for any convenient footage of blazing timber. One image would have been as serviceable as several dozen others. Instead of the precise but reverberating effects of the functioning image we would have observed a vamp-till-ready looseness of structure and connotation. Thus the *Potemkin* lion provides an outline of powerful and magical movement which we can fill with almost any thought, speculation or feeling at hand. More energy is spent on the assertion of meaning than is generated in its expression.

These objections to Eisenstein's usage seem valid and serious. But they are not presented as very damaging criticisms of either the director or his film; the lion image seems, rather, a momentary flaw – one of those bold but fruitless devices which adventurous film-makers are bound to explore. My quarrel is rather with those who have presented this device, and others like it, as models of creative editing, as support for the argument that cutting should be the major source of cinematic meaning, and to imply that the moments of greatest significance in a movie are those when the spectator is most violently alerted to the means by which significance is sought.

Attempts to employ editing as the unique, or massively dominant, source of meaning have a common tendency: they create image-patterns of some complexity at the expense of crudity in the images themselves. So much is surely inevitable. We cannot demonstrate that significance has been created solely by the interaction of images unless we first demonstrate that the images lack any significance of their own. The film-maker ensures that his effects derive from nothing but montage when, and only when, he takes care to drain all overtones of meaning from the constituent shots.

The classic theoretical instance of creative montage – the Kuleshov experiments reported by Pudovkin – depend absolutely upon this. Close-ups of an actor's face were combined with images of, in turn, a bowl of soup, a woman's corpse, and a playing child. The audience is said to have been enthusiastic about the actor's 'performance' of pensiveness, grief, and happiness respectively. Disregarding the uncontrolled nature of the experiment (how expectant, cooperative or discriminating was this audience?) it remains annoyingly specious to claim that shot one, 'man's face', plus shot two, 'woman in coffin', creates a *new* idea, 'man in grief'. We could expect the same idea to be communicable in a single shot of both man and corpse. Editing simply reinstates what was removed in the initial act of creation and selection, as Pudovkin confirms: 'we chose close-ups which were static and which did not express any feeling at all'. A damning indictment of theories derived from this report is implied by the fact that no one since Pudovkin has actually seen the film concerned. The volumes of discussion based on it thus assume from the start the irrelevance of all matters of lighting, make-up, camera angle and framing to the theoretical issues; assume, in fact, that the content of any specific presentation of a particular face is adequately described by the word 'face' or, worse still, 'close-up'.

I would wish the limits of my attack on montage theories to be clear. I claim only that there is no special merit attaching to the use of editing devices as such, and nothing more cinematic or creative about these usages than about achievements in the significant use of lighting, dialogue, décor, gesture or any other of the film-maker's resources. Equally there is no objection to the use of crude, single-meaning images as such. The cinema would be enormously the poorer if deprived of its loaded pistols, banana skins, ticking time-bombs and dripping taps. Basic to the synthetic approach to movies which I believe most productive is the claim that significance, emotional or intellectual, arises rather from the creation of significant relationships than from the presentation of things significant in themselves. Cutting certainly affords valuable facilities for the development of such relationships. I would, though, suggest that the more dense the network of meanings contained within each moment of film, the more richly these moments will combine and interact.

The shower-bath murder scene from *Psycho* may illustrate this view. Being entirely composed of fragments, it meets the requirements of the most convinced montagist. Many of its images, considered in isolation, seem to act as simple diagrams of objects and actions. Yet, restored to context, the sequence indicates the extraordinarily complex layers of interpenetrating meanings and effects that editing can offer the film-maker.

It is an indication of the strength of Hitchcock's conception and of the formal rigour of its execution that a full analysis of this scene could be given only as part of an analysis of the complete film. Here I shall offer no more than an outline of the sequence's structure and meaning. I shall not be able to examine even its cutting in detail. Length of shot and detailed context, the degree to which each image in its content, composition and movement reacts with its immediate neighbours – these important matters will be excluded from my discussion. But even a superficial treatment requires a sketch of the plot-situation for the benefit of the deprived few who have not seen the picture.

Marion Crane has driven away from the town where she has just robbed her employer's client of a large sum in cash. Exhausted by the long journey, and having lost her way in a rainstorm, she stops at a deserted motel, kept by Norman Bates, a painfully shy young man who looks after his intermittently insane mother in the house behind. Marion shares supper with Norman in his office next to her cabin. As a result of her conversation with him she decides to return the stolen money. Relieved of anxiety, she prepares for bed. As she undresses, Norman spies on her through a hole in the partition. After a few seconds he walks away angrily, as if intending to defy his mother's edict against bringing women into the house. Marion goes to the bathroom, steps into the shower and surrenders herself to its cleansing stream.

From this point the camera is – we are – inside the shower with Marion. Through the shower curtain we see the approach of a shadowy figure. The curtain is ripped aside to reveal, momentarily, the silhouette of a woman – Norman's mother. She hacks at Marion with a butcher's knife; walks away. Marion falls across the bath and dies.

Before we consider the precise imagery employed in the sequence, some part of the complexity of its treatment may be indicated by looking at the web of different purposes that is served by filming the murder as a montage of rapid close-ups.

At its most basic the depiction has to be stylized, because even Hitchcock's dedication does not sanction the slaughter of actresses. If make-up allowed the episode to be faked as a continuous piece of realistic action the sequence would be obscene.

More seriously, it would be nauseating. Hitchcock's treatment aestheticizes the horror, abstracting from reality so that we receive the most powerful and vivid *impression* of violence, brutality and despair. An extreme of intellectual and emotional shock is conveyed without provoking physical revulsion – which would detach us from the film. Marion's injuries are not shown; blood is not seen pulsing from her wounds. Similarly the sounds of attacker and attacked are supplanted by the scream of violins.

This treatment solves also the problem of viewpoint. So far in the film the spectator has shared Marion's consciousness almost exclusively. The shower scene starts with our seeing, for virtually the first time, something of which Marion is unaware: Norman's prying, during which we have in fact shared Norman's viewpoint. By its end Marion will be dead. So our identification with her must be released. Indeed it is a vital part of the design that we should be cut adrift emotionally by the shock removal of the picture's chief identification-figure, heroine and star. In the course of the scene, as our viewpoint jumps in violent agitation from place to place, we see less and less through Marion's eyes: and towards the end of the attack our viewpoint is more often the murderer's than the victim's.

The erratic viewpoint serves a further purpose: concealment. The film's end will reveal the murderer as Norman Bates, a psychopath who takes on the clothes and supposed identity of the long-dead mother whose corpse he has preserved. For the moment it is essential that we assume we have seen Norman's mother commit the murder. The brief shots of the attacking figure's outline serve to confirm this assumption while preventing us from inspecting the figure or realizing that the opportunity to inspect is being withheld.

Finally, Hitchcock's method allows him to maintain the impression of suddenness and violence whilst actually extending the duration of the incident on the screen. The two things, which seem contradictory, are in fact interdependent. We need time to appreciate the shock of the attack. Theoretically the entire murder could be depicted in a sustained shot of, for example, the arm wielding the knife. But it would be a very short time before this image lost its violence to become boring or ludicrous. The murder would have to be brought to an end at a point where, emotionally, it had just begun.

The fragmented, close-up treatment is justified as much by the confined setting as by its psychological-emotional aptness. A similar treatment would appear quite gratuitous if the murder occurred in a more open setting where the director was able but unwilling to move the camera back to show the complete action. Hitchcock demonstrates his 'helplessness' in one shot by placing his camera at ceiling height for the most distant view the setting permits.

But he is able to exploit a *scale* of distance, and of duration, in his images. It is not enough to say that the scene assembles brief fragments of action. Distinctions of length between the most and the least brief shots are strongly felt. A rhythm is established in which marginally slower cutting, as at the end with Marion's death-fall, presents a considerable *rallentando*. And within the range set by huge close-ups, like that of Marion's screaming mouth, there is room for violent change in the size of the image, even though the sequence contains nothing that would normally be regarded as a long shot. Film is a matter of relationships!

The images are of things which have a necessary existence in the scene *as things* and not only as projections of ideas and feelings. The purification of the imagery does not go so far that the images become detached from the events which it is their first function to depict. This incomplete purification is evident in the incomplete isolation of the scene's components: Marion's feet; the water; her blood; but also her blood mingling with the water flowing past her feet. Thus Marion's outspread fingers shown in close-up are not simply a visual configuration echoed elsewhere in the film but also and primarily her gripping, slipping wet hand sliding down the bathroom tiles. And the knife is first and foremost a knife, a meat knife, long, steely, sharply pointed and dull-edged.

Then, but only then, it is also a phallus, part of the scene's construction as symbolic rape. The knife is phallic on account not only of its accepted Freudian significance nor of the rhythm of its movement but also by relation to other shots – the vaginal imagery in the liquid, round shapes of (in close-up) the shower-rose, the drain and Marion's mouth. The scene is symbolic rape also in the context of the audience's expectation of a sexual encounter, an expectation provoked by Norman's prying, Marion's nakedness and her voluptuous surrender to the shower. It is significant of Hitchcock's integrity, his seriousness of artistic purpose in this highly sensational scene, that the imagery relates not to our suppositions about the action but to the real situation: Norman, possessed by *his* image of his mother, killing Marion in a cruel and pathetic parody of sexual contact. The knife-as-phallus also yields: Norman's manhood catastrophically manipulated by (a false image of) his mother.

The knife is also a bird's beak: in its swooping, pecking movement, with no moment of 'stick' or repose; and in relation to the forcefully presented images, earlier, of the stuffed birds which decorate Norman's parlour – night birds, birds of prey. The association, reinforced in the film's development, is again with Norman who animates the bird image as he animates 'mother'. Mother and birds alike are dead, sawdust-filled shells of past existences, living only the false life of Norman's tormented imagination. The knife-beak thus denotes the eruption of an illusory past into the reality of the present.

The knife's plunging diagonal contributes strongly to the

composition of movement, consistently downwards, towards the climax in Marion's fall. In this, the scene is part of the film's general movement. Each of the climaxes is built around a vertiginous descent which sweeps the audience farther downwards towards an abyss of darkness, madness, futility and despair. That is why the picture's final image, reversing this pattern – a brief shot of Marion's car being hauled up out of a swamp – carries such a powerful sensation of release.

Within the sequence the downward impetus is felt variously as crushing, being crushed, sinking, falling. It embodies the mad relentlessness of the assault and the ineluctable erosion of Marion's life. The scene's compositionally and emotionally most powerful elements – the knife, the flow of water, Marion's body and hand in their lurching slide down the tiled wall, the tearing and falling shower curtain – these are opposed only by Marion's will: her arm reaching out for the curtain's support asserts a momentary, tentative upward movement. But this is swiftly overruled by the curtain's collapse and Marion's fall.

The finality of her death is consummated in the image of the shower drain, seen in close-up with the swirling water sweeping her blood down into blackness. This image dissolves into a close-up of her eye in the unseeing stare of death. The sequence thus ends on a death-laden reversal of the living images with which it began. The water spraying from the shower rose has become the water plunging away down the drain. Norman's prying eye has become the dead stare of Marion's corpse. Here again the scene is pivotal. The eye motif prefigures the film's development towards both the blind gaze that will testify the ultimate annihilation of Norman's personality, and the absorption of his eyes into the sightless sockets of Mother's skull.

On the victim's behalf the downward movement further implies injustice (Marion's reaching for the curtain to halt her descent: an appeal against sentence of death) and degradation. This is especially relevant to *Marion's* knowledge that she is being slaughtered by a madman in a cheap wig. There is an element of the grotesque in the movement of the knife, like a spiteful child lashing out in a fit of temper; and in the image of Mother departing from the scene with a vindictively self-satisfied stomp, as if she had just had the last word in a silly neighbours' quarrel.

But as we see it through the eyes of the attacker the pounding descent is the crushing of a noxious body, elimination of an evil intruder, a punishment. The characterization of the murder in this way is an important part of the characterization of Norman's madness. It is achieved partly through the suggestion of ritual sacrifice in the image of the knife's first descent but also because we relate the killing and the assumed killer to Mother's accusing voice (overheard by Marion in the previous scene) and its vehement disgust at the cheap carnality of women's minds.

For the spectator as for Marion this 'punishment' is insanely disproportionate to either of her offences: desire or larceny. The more so since it immediately follows her decision to return the stolen money and is even inflicted at the very moment of her purification. We have already seen her 'wash her sins away' when she flushed down the lavatory the paper recording her financial calculations. The symbolic meaning of the shower-water, both for Marion and in Freudian formulation, is rebirth, a fresh start. Yet this very water becomes the knife's accomplice as a chief agent of her death, the means by which her life is 'drained away'. Its cleansing stream provides the décor for her defilement, its promise of forgiveness mocked and countermanded in vicious retribution. The stark ironies of this collision between symbolic meanings and experienced realities explode across a gaping chasm of futility.

The shower's symbolic effect is amplified by its further use as a visual replica. It reproduces the rain of an earlier scene. As Marion neared the end of her long journey her tired and anxious mind lurched from incriminating memory to guilty supposition. Driving down the night highway she imagined the outrage of the wealthy client, his impotent blustering at having been fooled and robbed by a pretty face. In her fantasy he was to vow to track her down and extract full value for the lost dollars from 'her fine, soft flesh'. Here, for the first time, Marion's haunted, hunted frown was broken by a smile of gleeful contempt. Immediately, we saw the car windscreen. The first drops of rain splashed across its surface, just as Marion's blood splashes on to the sides of the bath. The hiss of the ensuing downpour prefigured the noise of the shower-bath. The windscreen wipers swung back and forth across our vision in the rhythm of the knife. And Marion's eyes, dazzled by the oncoming headlights, stared blindly out into the blackness which finally revealed the Bates motel.

This ingeniously constructed sequence of pre-echoes makes Marion's punishment not more justified but less completely arbitrary. It becomes appropriate not to her actions but to her attitudes. She is destroyed by an explosion of forces existing within her own personality: the savage equation of sex and punishment, the self-comforting contempt for others' desires. 'The dirty old man deserved to lose his money' is a short step from 'The filthy slut deserves to lose her life'. It belongs to the same order of psychotic reasoning. Implicated as we have been in Marion's thought, we can not entirely refuse the guilt of Mother's action.

Hitchcock uses images from the murder scene as reference points by which to chart resemblances of attitude and action that link all his characters to Mother, to Norman's blindness and Norman's madness. Thus the windscreen-wiper/knife image culminates, at the final revelation of Mother's corpse, in the wildly swinging light-bulb that fills the skull's vacant sockets with a grotesque illusion of life. Even the most 'normal' of the film's characters, Marion's sister, is bound into the pattern. As she walks away round a corner during her investigation of the Bates motel her movement and Hitchcock's design create an image which precisely parallels that of Mother's exit from the murder scene.

It is a measure of the greatness of *Psycho*, and of Hitchcock at his finest, that the achievement of precise and densely interrelated imagery should seem to involve so little effort. Revealing moments accumulate without subjecting the drama to any apparent strain. It is only by thinking oneself into Hitchcock's position after the experience that one realizes what intensity of artistic effort must have been required. Which is to say, simply, that the effort of seeming effortless is the most demanding of all. How much easier, and how much more conclusively it would have established Hitchcock as a 'director with ideas', to have superimposed Mother's grinning skull on the smiling face of Marion at the steering-wheel.

Yet the absence of apparent effort depends on the director's ability to achieve his images and effects without reaching beyond the limits of the chosen action. There is a vital distinction between editing effects created out of dramatically relevant materials and those which are themselves the major reason for the materials' introduction. As against the *Potemkin* lions, which exist primarily or exclusively in order to be edited, Hitchcock's images of knife and water (like Brooks's of conflagration and Preminger's of Carmen and Joe in the jeep) would have to exist in the film in some form even if they were not to be used as components of a montage effect.

The inflection of Hitchcock's film towards the themes which preoccupy the director is a result of emphasis, not of superimposed statement. Some of the scene's meanings are inherent in our response to *any* naked female shower-bath knife-murder: obvious examples are degradation, violation, purification. But the director's treatment establishes the scale of our response, creates the priorities of feeling and meaning. For instance, it is clear that thoughts of physical pain are inseparable from the experience which we bring to the action. But Hitchcock does nothing to *activate* this response. Marion's agony, as we are made to experience it, is much more of the mind – of horror, shock and despair – than of the body. In our understanding of the scene, pain is relegated to a minimal role while other elements are promoted to major significance. Images and rhythm release those meanings which are most relevant to the director's purpose.

If this discussion has demonstrated the control over significance that editing offers to the director, it has also, I hope, shown that editing is a stylistic means rather than an aesthetic end. Quality and significance are not assessed in cuts-per-minute. Editing is simply one method among many of controlling a movie's organization. In *Psycho* it yields exactness of imagery and concentration of meaning, an intimately varied moment-by-moment command in the transmission of ideas and emotions. But elsewhere those same qualities have been achieved through the camera's prolonged stare from a distant viewpoint. The more a film benefits from rapid change of image, the less it can draw on the equally expressive possibilities of change *within* the image.

What matters is not how the image was derived from reality but how revealingly it relates to the movie's world. In this examination of the director's resources I have chosen to discuss significant but discreet uses of the medium, uses which neither leap out at us from the fictional world nor impose upon it a rhetoric that it cannot sustain. I hope to have indicated that such uses are the most productive in the fictional form with which we are concerned.

6 'How' Is 'What'

A persistent assumption in the previous chapter was that matters of balance and coherence are crucial to our appreciation of Cinema. I shall now try to justify this assumption and look at some of its most important implications.

Coherence is the prerequisite of meaning. It is the means by which the film-maker creates significance. The *spectator* employs a continuous coherence-test in order to recognize meaning at all levels. It is the means by which he *makes sense* of the images, the means by which he adjusts both his visual and his mental focus. At a certain brute level, that is clearly so: a patch of coloured light 'is' sea through its place in a network of relationships within the image which in turn relates to common experience outside the cinema.

While I have no wish to argue by sleight of hand from this brute level of consistency-dependence to my larger claim, it is not possible to make a clear distinction of kind between this and the higher or deeper levels. Does not a similar test, progressively refined, control recognition of that sea as background information incidentally necessary to the foreground action; as itself a focus of dramatic interest, the source, say, of likely danger or sustenance; as the symbolic representation of a state of mind, a wish, a fear, an impulse; finally, as suggesting an extension beyond the immediate concerns of character and action into the realm of ideas? How can that sea embody, say, human aspiration, unless through its relevance to figures whose aspirations we observe or share?

It can be made to do so, by the absolute negation of coherence. The sea image may be hurled into the movie with such aggressive disregard for dramatic relevance that our minds, intolerant of disjunction, search for conceivable connections and explore the symbolic connotations of Sea in quest of the one least tenuously related to the matters in hand. For it is certainly true that common experience and agreed usage have given objects a range of meanings quite independent of their presence in movie images; and that those meanings may readily be incorporated by pointing the camera appropriately. At its crudest, one could 'film' an idea by setting it down on paper and focusing on the printed page.

So my first statement on coherence needs amendment. Meaning may exist without internal relationship; but coherence is the prerequisite of *contained* significance. By this I mean significance which we find within, rather than attached to, the form of the film.

Despite my earlier reservations on the subject, the 'nature of the medium' is unavoidable if we want an aesthetic basis for critical judgements: the concept of the 'cinematic' needs thorough overhaul, but it cannot be abandoned. It is re-established as a critical tool, not just useful but necessary, once we pursue a definition which respects both the synthetic nature of the movie and the logic of its forms. The specifically filmic qualities derive from the *complex*, not from any one of its components. What distinguishes film from other media, and the fiction movie from other forms, is none of the elements but their combination, interaction, fusion.

The meanings which are contained most securely within a film are those formed at the deepest level of interrelation and synthesis. The point needs particular stress because it is only as we approach this level that it begins to make sense to talk of a film as self-contained in its significance. A movie cannot be both absolutely self-contained and meaningful. It draws non-stop on the values and knowledge which we bring to it. Recognition and interpretation of the film's experience both depend on an immediate responsiveness at the level where meaning is *given* rather than created.

The kitchen scene from *The Courtship of Eddie's Father*, for example, refers out to our awareness of, among other things, the fragility of china, the uncertain stability of a high stool, and

American assumptions about the proper roles and interests of parents. These given meanings are essential to the significance of the scene. But as components only. The special concern of the movie is to put such components into significant relationship; their correlation is the content of the film.

Our understanding and judgement of a movie, then, will depend largely on the attempt to comprehend the nature and assess the quality of its created relationships. We are mistaken if we persuade ourselves that one film is more subtle or profound than another on the grounds that its typical reference points include data drawn from the philosophy of Hegel or the poetry of Goethe rather than from conventions of dress or fashion in motor transport. The subtlety, complexity or intelligence of a picture is not to be found in its given meanings. These qualities may be seen in its organization; they should not be claimed for (nor should naïvety, crudity or triviality be charged against) isolated units.

If we agree in making qualities of organization and coherence a primary issue in critical judgement, complexity and subtlety are vindicated as highly relevant criteria. But they are so for *aesthetic* reasons, and not because complex views or statements are generally preferable to simple ones. Complexity of viewpoint requires and justifies elaborated expression. But the simpler statements under-employ a complex medium. They need only the diagrammatic relationship of a few givens to yield significance at a level we could call that of *asserted* meaning. At this level coherence exists but lacks density. In bald oppositions like those between palaces and slums, battlefields and stock-markets, we find generalized images joined to create approximations to verbal messages. Film becomes a substitute for speech, a translation of verbal statements, rather than an alternative, independent mode of communication.

A movie whose significance is restricted to the message-making level competes in an area where images are markedly less efficient than words. Less efficient because less clear. If we wish to transmit a verbal message it makes little sense to interpose unnecessary coding and de-coding stages between sender and receiver. We simply create additional opportunities for 'interference' and distortion. The *Potemkin* lions have already provided an example of the imprecision which descends upon attempts to make images do the work of slogans or verbal metaphors.

Asserted meanings, crude juxtapositions, tend to be both blatant and unclear, like over-amplified noises bellowing from a faulty loudspeaker. When a film's significance is wholly formed at this level it is better described as *imposed* than as contained. This description will indicate its status as meaning which is created by the superficial effort of organization involved in such manoeuvres as using a character as the mouthpiece for a speech.

Not that there is any law which bars characters from speaking their thoughts. Far from it. Density of coherence, by its nature, cannot be instantly achieved. A level of asserted meaning is an indispensable stage between the setting out of givens and the creation of a complex structure. Many fine movies *start* from simple propositions and crude confrontations. Thus *Ugetsu Monogatari* is built from a schematic opposition of misery and ambition, devastation and toil. *La Règle du jeu* opens with a blatant juxtaposition of modern technology and romantic chivalry. In *Johnny Guitar* and *Carmen Jones*, the initial relationships between solidarity and isolation, freedom and enclosure, are boldly outlined.

Asserted meanings cannot be ignored; but equally they should not be overvalued. What matters is the extent to which these bold statements are refined by the pattern of detail built over and around them. In any of the films listed above we find subtlety and complexity not (where it's nonsensical to look for them) in the initial scheme, but in an organization of details whose relationships simultaneously complicate and clarify the movie's viewpoint. At this level of coherence significance is locked into the picture's form. We are taken beyond the realm of the language substitute which provides an *illustration* of messages, opinions and themes. The separately discernible meanings become important less for their independent value than for their contributions, mutually deepening and defining, to a total vision.

What we see here is, primarily, a way of seeing; the direct

registration and embodiment, in a 'secondary world', of a point of view. Our approach to the significance of this world is through the subtle laws which structure its relationships. But the following would be as true, and perhaps closer to the nub of the matter: significance provides the path by which we approach and seek to make manageable the intricacies of structure.

The cinema offers no difficulties to our perception and judgement, and no challenge to the film-maker when it sets out to employ only one of its resources. Critical and creative problems arise from the attempt to balance requirements of equal weight but divergent tendency. Useful criteria take account of relatedness by directing us not to single aspects but to the value of their interaction and the extent of their integration. The formal disciplines of balance and coherence embrace the effort to maintain the various elements in productive tension and neither to push them into symmetrical alignment (repetition) nor to let them fall into blank contradiction.

Friction impedes movement; at the same time movement is impossible without friction. By a similar paradox the film-maker finds a degree of resistance in his material which both provides and restricts the channel of communication. Resistance offers a principle of tension by which to locate his work within the secure frame of reference on which internal relationship depends.

Certainly the spectator needs such a frame in order to perceive relationship. But the need, and the means of supplying it, arise from the same source: the hybrid nature of film, the synthesis of reality and magic implied by the cinema's basic mechanism.

The movie is committed to finding a balance between equally insistent pulls, one towards credibility, the other towards shape and significance. And it is threatened by collapse on both sides. It may shatter illusion in straining after expression. It may subside into meaningless reproduction presenting a world which is credible but without significance.

The meanings I attach to the word 'significance' are, I trust, clear. But in a context where people are known to burst into song on the tops of trolley-buses, with the full support of invisible orchestras, or sprint down hillsides actively pursued by bouncing boulders, or drag wild leopards determinedly up the steps of Connecticut jails (and I would be the last to suggest they cease exhibiting such fine accomplishments), the concept of credibility needs careful definition. As an illusion-spinning medium, film is not bound by the familiar, or the probable, but only by the conceivable. All that matters is to preserve the illusion.

On one level cinematic credibility is no different from that which we demand of other story-telling forms. It depends on the inner consistency of the created world. So long as that is maintained, the premises are beyond question: people can express their feelings in impromptu song, with or without instrumental backing; inanimate objects can be self-willed and malevolent; Death can be a devotee of chess. But the created world must obey its own logic. There is no pretext, whether it be Significance, Effect or the Happy Ending, sufficient to justify a betrayal of the given order. In a fictional world where anything at all can happen, nothing at all can mean or matter.

This fact has specific implications for the movie. It gives the criterion of credibility a *physical* dimension which it has not had elsewhere in art since the decline of representational painting. Faced with the camera's obstinate literal-mindedness (which means our literal-minded approach to the camera's products), the film-maker follows Conrad's advice to the drowning man: 'In the destructive element immerse . . .' Conquest through submission: since the image insists on its relationship with visual reality, the film-maker takes that as one of the starting points for his organization and works through it to achieve reality for his imagined world. In this sense even the fiction movie is a documentary – the Authentic Record brought back from a fictional universe.

Here too it is important that we avoid confusing credibility with authenticity. The question of authenticity simply does not arise when we enter a fictional world. There is no actuality against which we can check images derived from *One Million Years B.C.* or *2001*. But the image must be credibly derived from the created world in order to maintain its reality.

A very basic demonstration of the two levels of credibility is provided by Hitchcock's *The Birds*. On the first level, we can make no difficulty about the fact that the feathered kingdom is seen to declare war on humanity. That is given. But it is also given that the attackers are ordinary, familiar birds. Nothing in our experience or in the film's premises permits them to develop intermittent outlines of luminous blue as they swoop, or to propel themselves in a manner that defies the observable laws of winged flight.

While it was scarcely Hitchcock's fault if his movie's central hypothesis was weakened by the fallibility of Special Effects, other directors have voluntarily incurred a similar breakdown, most often by forcing their actors into unconvincing postures or movements in order to fit a preconceived image. The more aspiring among inept film-makers frequently do this in pursuit of Dramatic Impact, which is like cutting off one's nose to beautify one's face.

Nothing the *camera* does can offer any threat to the credibility of the imagined world. It has complete freedom, within that world, to seek its most revealing image. It can hang from the ceiling, look through kaleidoscopes, coloured filters or distorting lenses, and register with varying degrees of definition, grain and focus.

But we make sense of the movie image by *relating* it to our common knowledge and experience of the visible world. The relationship cannot be one of simple correspondence. In the colour movie, for example, the prominence or absence of particular tones may be thoroughly abnormal or designedly unnatural: no part of the greatness of a Western like *Johnny Guitar* or a musical like *The Pirate* could be traced to the likelihood of their colour-schemes. An apparent artificiality of décor in no way undermines the kind of belief assumed by *The Wizard of Oz*.

In *Moulin Rouge* John Huston established (and exploited with, for the most part, enthralling results) a system of colour based on the palettes of the Impressionists and therefore owing nothing to naturalism. Yet he had not created a world whose reality could tolerate a room that changed colour in sympathy with its occupant's moods. When the director characterized his hero's jealousy by flooding the set with, in the film's own terms, inexplicable green light, he broke down the essential structure of his picture's relationships and thus destroyed the world within which his hero *existed*. A minor, momentary relationship between the hero's temper and a literary convention of colour ('green with envy') was surely not worth achieving – or, more strictly speaking, capable of being achieved – at the sacrifice of the fundamental pattern. Here, as in my earlier examples from *The Red Desert* and *The Criminal*, the short cut is seen to create a short-circuit.

No game worth watching changes its rules at the players' convenience. From the spectator's point of view, part of the function of the narrative discipline is to prevent the story-teller's making things easy for himself at the expense of his work. But while a coherent principle of organization is essential, it is not in itself enough. A game may be played in strict accordance with a consistent body of rules yet remain a dull game. The rules provide a basis, not a substitute, for skilled and exciting play.

In like manner the disciplines of credibility adopted by the film-maker can be of only partial help to our understanding and judgement. By enabling us to explain why some part of a movie's structure is incoherent they allow us to indicate that the work is flawed; how seriously flawed will depend on how marginal or central the incoherence proves to be. But when we've said that a film is credible, we've not said much. We have established the soundness at only one end of its balance.

I have now described both sides of this balance, credibility as well as significance, in terms of coherence. But as the *Moulin Rouge* example has shown, the relationships concerned are of different kinds. The problem of balance arises because different relationships may make incompatible demands. When that happens opposed strains lead not to productive tension but to breakdown.

The image too has its givens. Like the created world, and in harmony with it, the image retains its sense and validity so long as it follows the logic of its premises. We can adjust to any scheme of selection provided that it is appreciable as a scheme. In coming to terms with the cinema's artifice we need to be able to sense which elements of our common experience apply and which are in suspension. The credibility of an artificial world, the reliability of an artificial eye, depend on the consistency of their relationship with our reality and on a system of deviation from the norms of our experience.

In the photographic film tension is applied whenever the image is required to act not just as representation but also as a significant structure. The relationship between image and thought may conflict with or reinforce that between image and object. As the weight of meaning carried by the image increases, so does the strain placed on this balance. At any point short of collapse, the tension is a source of strength and energy. Up to this point, the greater the force of expression which the image can be seen to bear, the more illuminating will be the interlock between what is shown and the way of showing it.

The movie's technical conventions allow the film-maker himself to define the principles of organization which are to control this relationship. When we enter the cinema we have to accept the implications of a controlled viewpoint. Since the camera has no brain, it has vision but not perception. It is the film-maker's task to restore the selectivity of the cinematic eye. In this process he may control our perception so that *his* vision and emphases dominate our response to the created world.

A scene in *Rope* demonstrates how extensively the controlled viewpoint may heighten our response to action without making our awareness of control a barrier to imaginative involvement. The two murderers have placed their victim's corpse in an unlocked chest. At their dinner party refreshments are served from the top of the chest-coffin. The books which are usually kept in the chest have been placed in the next room. After dinner the housekeeper begins to clear the chest. When she has finished doing so she will want to replace the books. She makes three journeys to and from the dining-room, taking away empties and bringing back books. Throughout this deliberately extended scene the camera stands fixed so that we can watch her going about her perilous business. We know where the young criminals and their guests are standing, we can hear their conversation, but we can see only the back of one of the guests at the very edge of the screen.

Hitchcock has deliberately chosen an angle which prevents us from seeing either of his guilty heroes. The suspense of the scene depends on our being made to wait for the moment when the housekeeper opens the chest. It is heightened by the frustration of our desire to know whether either of the heroes is in a position to observe what is happening and so intervene to prevent catastrophe. The effect depends on a calculated refusal of desired information.

A similar refusal of information occurs in William Wyler's *The Loudest Whisper*. We are shown a schoolgirl telling her strait-laced grandmother a scandalous lie about the relationship between two of her teachers. However, we do not hear the accusation because at the moment the child begins to speak Wyler cuts in a shot from the front seat of the car in which they are travelling. The glass panel behind the chauffeur prevents our hearing the rest of the conversation. The obvious intention is to heighten the menace of the scene, to emphasize the 'unspeakable' nature of the charge. There is no need for us to hear the actual words spoken since we are well enough aware that the accusation is of homosexuality.

Both Hitchcock and Wyler in these scenes are exploiting the opportunities created by the necessity of a controlled viewpoint to heighten our response by providing only a partial 'view' of the action. In each case the alert spectator is likely to be aware of the device employed to secure the effect. Yet I would maintain that there is a great disparity between the strength and validity of the two devices.

When Wyler changes our viewpoint he quite clearly does so at his own convenience and at our expense. The camera changes position only in order to explain the silence; the effect is scarcely more subtle than a simple cut-out on the sound-track. The change of angle covers the silence, but gives us no new or interesting information which would justify the change itself. There is, literally, no excuse for the device: we are deprived of what we expected to hear and offered no compensatory distraction. We are thus encouraged to notice the nature of the device, at the expense of the response which it was too clearly designed to provoke.

But in *Rope* the effect of the restrictive viewpoint is in no way damaged by our awareness of the director's design. What we are prevented from seeing is fully covered by what we do see and know. The position of the guests at one side of the room was established naturalistically *before* the housekeeper began her clearing up; as so often in Hitchcock's work, the fact is initially offered as a piece of neutral, more or less irrelevant information so that it is not questionable later, when it takes on its more threatening aspect. We could still object to the camera device if Hitchcock had not employed his décor so cunningly. He has placed his actors in such a way that within this setting there is no angle from which the camera could embrace both the corner where the heroes are standing and the housekeeper's passage from sitting-room to dining-room. In order to stand back far enough to include both points the camera would have to travel, and see, through the wall opposite the sitting-room door. If this episode occurred early in the film we might suspect that the wall, like Wyler's glass panel, served only the purpose of restricting our knowledge. But the camera has explored the apartment so freely in the preceding sequences that by the time Hitchcock begins to exploit his décor for dramatic effect we have come to accept its reality and the limitations which it imposes. We cannot, at this stage, see the décor as something which exists purely at the director's convenience in order to inhibit the camera and limit our access to the action.

Hitchcock's cunning makes him seem to be a victim of the situation at just the point where he is most completely its master. The scene has been moulded so that, whatever happens, we shall be able to see only *one* of the focal points of its drama: *either* the housekeeper and the chest *or* the heroes. If the camera were to move to show the heroes we would lose sight of the housekeeper; as long as its eye remains fixed on the housekeeper we are unable to see the heroes. Hitchcock's camera is obsessively concerned with the menace of the housekeeper's actions. It 'can't take its eyes off her'. But the same presentation, just as skilfully integrated, would seem ridiculous applied to an event of less gravity: if, for example, the chest was known to contain only the evidence of some minor indiscretion and not the corpse of a man who was son, nephew, pupil, best friend and fiancé to the various guests.

The emphasis provoked by Hitchcock's confined viewpoint is consonant with the dramatic import of the action it shows. This cannot be claimed for Wyler's glass silencer; the action here is not sufficiently 'charged' to bear the weight of meaning which the scale of the device asserts.

Emphasis depends on the establishment of a norm. In the fictional film the norm is given by the nature of the spectator's relationship to narrative. Our relationship to stories is that of an interested observer – the satisfaction they offer depends upon the extent to which they arouse concern. Once our interest in a story is aroused our drive is to discover *what happens*. So it is the structural information, the facts which indicate possibilities of development and resolution, that we grasp first and with most ease. When we have grasped the available structural information our perception of less specifically functional information increases.

With reference to this characteristic the film-maker establishes his norm, a base from which he can move in order to assign degrees of importance to objects and events within his world. While each film-maker establishes his own base, he does so by reference to a standard expectation. As 'interested observers' we expect the image to be the ideal record; freed from human contingencies, its attention is devoted to the matter of greatest moment for *us*.

Since the spectator expects the image to operate as a clear presentation of necessary facts, he is able to comprehend its other functions by sensing the import of deviations from the norm. The anticipation of relevant information in the image provokes close attention, in part at least because despite the 'perfection' of the record we can never be certain whether information which appears merely contingent may turn out to be structurally vital. When the amount of clearly relevant information is reduced, our attention may be directed towards a more intense scrutiny of the less extensive and less active images. We are provoked to assume an enhanced relevance in what we *do* see because it is given a special status in the film's world, an emphasis that implies heightened significance.

The degree of deviation from the norm indicates the scale of emphasis assigned by the film-maker. The less completely the image is committed to offering us information about developments in the film's world, the more it asserts its own significance either as a particularly revealing view of that world or as a presentation of a particularly significant aspect.

The controlled viewpoint presupposes a continuous quest for the most revealing presentation of events. But it remains open to the film-maker to heighten or subdue our awareness of his control. We can be made more or less conscious that we are seeing the world through a particular 'eye'. That is why it is possible for the film-maker to establish emphasis from his own base and in his own way. For Otto Preminger

the ideal picture is a picture where you don't notice the director, where you never are aware that the director did anything deliberately. Naturally he has to do everything deliberately – that is direction. But if I could ever manage to do a picture that is directed so simply that you would never be aware of a cut or a camera movement, that, I think, would be the real success of direction.[1]

This 'real success' is unattainable, at least so far as the alert spectator is concerned. Ironically, one of the major pleasures of a Preminger movie is the grace and fluidity of his camera movements. But Preminger's ideal picture makes sense as an aspiration which reflects one attitude to the spectator and one type of viewpoint. Preminger uses means of emphasis which do not draw our attention to the image as an image but rely on arranging the action so that the scale of significance is established *there*. In *River of No Return* the symbolism is so completely absorbed into the action that it may easily pass unnoticed. When the heroine drops most of her belongings into the water as she is lifted from a raft grounded on the rapids, the camera does nothing to emphasize

1. Otto Preminger in *Movie* magazine, No. 4, p. 20.

the meaning of the incident. It could be seen, at best, as a demonstration of the dangerous power of the current (her bag hurtles away downstream); at worst, it might look like mere padding designed to keep the action moving along for a few extra seconds. In either case a claim that the event has symbolic significance would seem an absurd and pretentious exercise in 'reading-in'.

Still, the claim is made. The loss of the bag is the first in a series of events which, in the course of her journey, strip the heroine of the physical tokens of her former way of life. This process parallels the character's moral development from fatalistic acceptance towards a degree of self-conscious decision. The two movements are united in the final shot of the movie: the heroine herself removes and throws away a pair of flashy red shoes, her last remaining item of 'uniform'.

The fact that the bag is lost to the rushing waters is itself significant. Contrasted attitudes to the river point up different attitudes to life; the heroine initially regards it as an irresistible force of nature, but to the hero it is a force which must be mastered, used and, when necessary, defied. The first time we see Robert Mitchum in relation to the river he is riding along the bank in the opposite direction to that of the current. But our first sight of Marilyn Monroe on the river shows her as its victim, swept along helplessly on a raft she cannot control.

Preminger reveals significance by a dramatic structuring of events which his camera seems only to follow – never to anticipate. Moreover, the image appears to attempt always to accommodate the entire field of action so that it is the spectator's interest which defines the area of concentration.

At the other end of the scale Hitchcock is prepared to indicate areas of concentration very forcibly. The chest-clearing scene from *Rope* impresses on us the fact that our view is partial and that the area of our concentration has been defined by the director. Hitchcock allows us no independent selection. Moreover, he is fully prepared to use a camera which anticipates the action. The shot which follows the heroine's plea for help in *Marnie* is a camera movement towards a door, the very deliberation of which predicts an event of crucial significance.

The distinction between these two approaches is necessarily one of degree. Hitchcock's ability to impose an area of interest is contingent upon that area's being or quite rapidly becoming as important to us as his treatment assumes. Preminger's open image imposes on us *his* sense of foreground and background; obviously a certain anticipation of events is inherent in the movement from sequence to sequence. While neither of these tendencies can be observed in a pure state, in Hitchcock the norm is a base for meaningful deviation while Preminger works by accumulation, enriching the basic structure by the addition of detail whose significance the spectator is free to observe or ignore. The contrast between their methods is further reflected in their narrative styles. Hitchcock tells stories as if he knows how they end, Preminger gives the impression of witnessing them as they unfold. Employed without skill, Preminger's method would be dull and unrevealing; Hitchcock's would be bombastic.

What matters to our judgement of the 'Hitchcock tendency' is not that an assertion of significance is made, but that we can feel it to be justified. Then the correlation of emphasis assigned with importance perceived maintains the authority of the image. It creates stress without strain by winning our acceptance of the given viewpoint.

The fictional world is not some inert matter to be galvanized into significance by the rhetorical manipulation of the movie's language. The trouble with Wyler's usage in *The Loudest Whisper* is that it places too great a reliance on the independent value of a technical device as a source of impact and meaning. We can claim that it 'uses the medium', but larger claims for a productive relationship of viewpoint and event can be advanced only when the film-maker maintains the correspondence between stylistic and dramatic weight.

In his own interest the film-maker must protect the channel through which his personal vision becomes communicable, the terms from which it derives its sense, strength and clarity. The more urgent his desire to communicate, the more persistently is he likely to be tempted to go beyond those terms in order to heighten meaning and impact. But when he disrupts his established discipline, in however worthy a cause, he is like a mason digging away his foundations to quarry stone for a steeple.

The hallmark of a great movie is not that it is without strains but that it absorbs its tensions; they escape notice until we project ourselves into the position of the artist and think through the problems which he confronted in his search for order and meaning. The more each element is not just compatible with, but an active contributor to, the network of significant relationships, the more value we can claim for the synthesis achieved.

Here the details of the realization will reveal concentration of function and effect. That is what distinguishes the examples of film-craft which I have held up for admiration; they achieve simultaneous relevance on the planes of action, thought and feeling. Cause and effect become inseparable because the aspect that exists in its own right stands also in a productive relationship: speech to gesture to décor (*The Courtship of Eddie's Father*); action to image to cutting (*Carmen Jones*); event to location to lighting to mood (*Rebel Without a Cause*). At such levels of integration no question arises whether the camera moves to accommodate the movements of the characters or the characters move to justify the movement of the camera (*The Cardinal, Rope*); whether the décor takes on meaning because of the action within it or whether it is the décor that makes actions meaningful (*Johnny Guitar, River of No Return*). Questions like these become pure chicken and egg.

The great film approaches an intensity of cohesion such that its elements do not operate solely to maintain or further the reality of the fictional world, nor solely to decorative, affective or rhetorical effect. Of course this is a counsel of perfection, even though it is one derived from existing movies. *Exodus, Johnny Guitar, Letter from an Unknown Woman, Psycho, La Règle du jeu, Rio Bravo, Wild River*: these are among the films which I recall as approaching this condition most closely. Yet each of them *does* contain actions and images whose sole function is to maintain the narrative. In most cases these moments are to be found during the initial exposition; in *Psycho*, notably and on account of its peculiar construction, they occur at the end. But these masterpieces allow us reasonably to hope for the next best thing to total cohesion: minimum (credible) redundancy. And they remind us that the minimum can be minute.

To hope for the fewest possible one-function elements in a film is not to demand that every element be of *equal* significance. There is a modulation of scale within each image just as there is throughout the whole movie. While we may expect each action to be relevant, only some will be climactic. One of the advantages of the narrative 'frame' is that the relevance of details to theme and viewpoint is a variable; it may occasionally be relaxed without threatening the overall coherence of the film.

Yet the movie that contains too much material serving only to maintain its reality pays the penalty of slackness and dullness, occasional or total. An even higher price is paid for unattached decoration, emotion or assertion: in vacuity, sentimentality or pretension. If I have said little in this chapter about such traditional failings – or about the traditional qualities like inventiveness, wit and economy – it is not because I think them unimportant. Rather, because they result from defects or achievements of balance and integration, and are most clearly defined in those terms. What, after all, is sentimentality if not a failure of emphasis, a disproportion between pathos asserted (in music, say, or image or gesture) and pathos achieved, in the action? What is pretension other than an unwarranted claim to significance, meaning insecurely attached to matter? And what inventiveness, but the ability to create the most telling relationships within the given material?

How can economy be defined unless by parity between energy expended and effect conveyed? 'Energy' itself is a matter of scale: a fast camera movement will *claim* most in a predominantly static movie; a big close-up will hit hardest in a picture mainly composed of more distant images. Consider again the *Psycho* slaughter. I have already talked of the concentration of imagery that Hitchcock's fragmented treatment allowed. It is equally valid to remark that without such concentration, the treatment would have fallen quite flat. If the emotional intensity of the scene's action *permits* extreme imagery, it is also largely a consequence of it. The correspondence between action, image, meaning and effect is so tight that each maintains the others. In theory, for example, Hitchcock could have given a more detached image at a number of points by moving the camera back through the open door of the bathroom. But the more distant view would have been quite inapposite to our experience of the action. The limitation of space was not entirely physical; it corresponded also to a psychological-emotional enclosure.

Hitchcock's achievement here represents as well as may be the achievement of any fine film-maker working at his peak. He does not let us know whether he is finding the style to suit his subject or has found the subject which allows him best exercise of his style. He builds towards situations in which the most eloquent use of his medium cannot emerge as bombast.

At the level of detail we can value most the moments when narrative, concept and emotion are most completely fused. Extended and shaped throughout the whole picture, such moments compose a unity between record, statement and experience. At this level too, sustained harmony and balance ensure that the view contained in the pattern of events may be enriched by the pattern of our involvement. When such unity is achieved, observation, thought and feeling are integrated: film becomes the projection of a mental universe – a mind recorder.

Synthesis here, where there is no distinction between how and what, content and form, is what interests us if we are interested in film as film. It is that unity to which we respond when film as fiction makes us sensitive to film as film.

7 Participant Observers

In the cinema style reflects a way of seeing; it embodies the film-maker's relationship to objects and actions. But, as a way of *showing*, it also involves his relationship with the spectator. The film's point of view is contained within each of these relationships. Attitudes towards the audience contribute as much to a movie's effect, and therefore its significance, as attitudes towards its more immediate subject-matter.

In the (ideally) comforting, self-forgetting darkness of the movie-house we attain faceless anonymity, a sort of public privacy, which effectively distances the real world and our actual circumstances. That the darkness is an essential insulator will have been realized by any reader who has had to watch films in an insufficiently darkened cinema. The deterioration of the image on the screen matters far less than the absence of the 'shield' which darkness customarily offers. The erection of the shield seems to be the precondition of involvement.

The rituals of film presentation acknowledge this fact by allowing the spectator time at the beginning and end of the movie to shed and reassume his self-consciousness. The final shot in most pictures is designedly recessional. An overwhelming majority of movies closes on some variation of the cliché which has hero and heroine walking arm in arm away from the camera (the audience) and towards the sunset. The apparent distance between the spectator and the characters on the screen is steadily increased, and the physical withdrawal detaches us psychologically, or helps us to detach ourselves, from the illusion. The end shot, however it is accomplished, is usually held long enough to lose some of its interest. Our involvement is considerably diminished by the time the house lights come up. If the film has been at all gripping, the effect is rather like a gradual return to consciousness after sleep.

These remarks make no claim for originality. But they have seemed worth setting down again because, obvious as they may be in themselves, they are usually presented with pejorative or at least patronizing implications. Film studios become 'dream-factories'. Most movies are said to offer 'vicarious experience' and this, it is assumed but seldom stated, makes them as negligible for the critic as they are fascinating for the social-psychologist. 'Dream-world', 'illusory', 'vicarious', 'manufactured', 'escapist', 'synthetic', 'second-hand' – all these expressions, while describing accurately many aspects of our experience in the cinema, have acquired a contemptuous ring. They seem to place movies on the same level as alcohol, or tobacco and narcotics, or religion, or gambling, or any of the other real or alleged opiates by means of which we withdraw from the realities of life.

The psychologist Erich Fromm included film-going with day-dreaming as activities equally harmful in distracting us from our real problems. C. Day Lewis in his 'Overtures to Death' extended the following sardonic invitation:

> Enter the dream-house, brothers and sisters, leaving
> Your debts asleep; your history at the door:
> This is the home for heroes, and this loving
> Darkness a fur you can afford.

In his book *Film World*, Ivor Montagu equated the mass-public movie with 'bingo and bowls (which) provide athletics for non-athletes'. It was 'a drug once, twice, more times a week'. Montagu was in no doubt that most people went to films seeking escape from the pitiful futility of their everyday lives. 'Often,' he said,

it [discontent] is the belief that it [happiness] could be achieved by luck, if only the cards had fallen the other way, or else it is nothing so definite that it could quite be called any belief, and then in either case, it is more apt to lead to a feeling of frustration, grumbling and going to the cinema.[1]

These words came the more surprisingly from Mr Montagu

1. Ivor Montagu, *Film World*, pp. 221, 220, 218.

because he was himself at one time concerned in the production of some notable and popular pictures. However, in his contempt for the 'dream-palace', he was simply following a line established by the orthodox defenders of the movie's art status. An object of the standard manuals of film appreciation has been to increase the detachment with which we view the screen. The movies may in most cases be manufactured and consumed as escapist entertainment; but the true 'Art of the Film', we are assured, is found elsewhere than in 'the commercial dream-incarnation formula'.

'Identification,' says Montagu,

happens smoothly without any effort on [the spectator's] part, he has only to sit back, relax, revel in the warmth, the music, the upholstery, the focus of attention out of dimness into a wavering bright light in the centre – all particularly conducive to submission to Svengali. . . . Those who want more solid food are sometimes found undergoing the rigours of hard benches that keep their senses alert.[2]

I know of no more succinct reassertion, in terms of cinema, of the old notion that virtue consists in hardship, and that what's pleasant must be regarded with suspicion. Naturally, the view which values art as a form of flagellation precludes the acceptance of effortless enjoyment. Movies can be worthwhile only when they provide an intellectual means-test. As I stated in my first chapter, the battle for the cinema's cultural status has been won. But it was a Pyrrhic victory to the extent that it was won at the cost of rigidifying a distinction between film as art-object and movie as vicarious experience. Up to a certain point, the volume of intellectual activity overtly required to comprehend a picture has become a standard by which its quality is assessed. But the fiction movie normally discourages awareness that we are interpreting its images and disguises the fact that it is a created object. The more successful it is, the smaller its chances of winning approval from those whose major pleasure in the cinema comes from intellectual gratification; it *must* be unacceptable to the man whose demand is for films which flatter his IQ by allowing him satisfactorily to decode the 'message'. Mr Montagu's book illustrates this point perfectly in

2. ibid., p. 219.

its equal contempt for any picture which aims either below or above its author's own level: films are patronized as frivolous when they do not demand an effort of comprehension, and condemned as meaningless when they require greater resources than the author commands. ('Alain Resnais has developed a technique of the portentous so obscure that no one [*sic*] can tell what anything portends.'[3]) Mental exercise is certainly one of the cinema's pleasures. 'Chase the meaning' is an enjoyable game, but it is not our only legitimate satisfaction. Films are not solely, or chiefly, valuable as crossword puzzles in which the clues are difficult enough to make their solution gratifying, but not so difficult as to frustrate solution altogether.

Such an attitude considers the film-dream only in its negative aspects, as an alternative, not an addition, to our real lives. Too strong an emphasis on what the movies allow us to escape *from* (the rain, overcrowded houses, financial problems or whatever) distracts us from the more positive function of escapism, ignores the importance of what we escape *into*. Films cannot simply erase reality; if they do not offer us a substitute experience we return to our real environment as people who have paid to sit disconsolately in *this* seat, in *this* cinema, at *this* time when we could have stayed at home and performed other more useful or pleasurable tasks.

Some of this is admitted or condoned by the sternest of our puritans. Involvement and vicarious experience are necessary to the notion of catharsis and eminently respectable in that context. There seems to be no difficulty in recognizing that we can profit from experiences, however second-hand, which are to some extent unpleasant. Pleasure-in-pain seems to be more readily accepted than pleasure in pleasure. 'The end of poetry', in Johnson's well-known definition, 'is to instruct by pleasing.' Films often seem to upset the balance of pleasure and instruction. Our experience becomes so diverting that the possibility of an underlying profundity is too easily dismissed. And pleasure, despised, ceases to please. The trouble with movies is that they so often provide a gratifying experience. A picture need not rise far above the level of competence in order to involve us. To distinguish movies which

3. ibid., p. 290.

succeed in maintaining involvement is discrimination at the lowest level of efficiency.

It is at this level that movies are judged both by the uncritical escapist and by the (apparently) hypercritical enemy of escapism; in both views, one dream is as good – or as bad – as another. Both parties ignore, through naïvety or prejudice, the possibility of a more sophisticated discernment because both regard the dream as inherently insignificant.

Movies often present a clumsily, cynically contrived exercise in simple wish-fulfilment. But 'second-hand' experience *can* be shared experience. The illusory world which we enter may reflect the film-maker's vision of the world. The experience which we undergo in the cinema may be his experience of life. Our dream can be his reality. Film is distinguished by the directness with which the experience, the vision, is presented. There seems to be no intermediate stage between the artist's statement and our reaction. We are not aware of 'reading' the image. No act of interpretation, no effort of imagination or comprehension seems needed. It's all there in front of us. Film narrative bypasses description. We react directly to instantaneous visual presentation, to event, character and place.

Direct response allows direct communication. The facility, the immediacy of our reactions is essential to this degree of involvement. Without apparent effort of will or imagination, and without conscious adjustment of our attitudes, we can share points of view, ways of seeing, which are foreign to us. Films can make us associate with attitudes which are not our own, with thoughts, feelings and reactions which are outside our normal range. Within limits the film-maker can recast our normal priorities of response. Vicarious experience can bring us a valuably extended experience and a broadened range of sympathies, but it cannot be isolated from our more active pleasures. Our involvement with personalities and in actions is only one part of a much wider and more complex experience.

Jean-Luc Godard, provoked by a Preminger movie to contemplate the 'mystery and fascination' of the American cinema, asked himself how he could 'hate John Wayne upholding Goldwater and love him tenderly when abruptly he takes Natalie Wood into his arms in the next-to-last reel of *The Searchers*'. His question takes us much closer to the essential issues than the traditional model of the 'film-dream' which depends upon unlikely assumptions about the spectator's relationship to film narrative. In that model, the basic form of the film-dream is the shape of a fantasy, fear or desire located in 'identification', built to its maximum intensity and at last fulfilled.

The analogy with dream and the concept of identification are useful only when they are treated with caution. In its strictest application the concept of identification refers to a relationship which is impossible in the cinema – namely an unattainably complete projection of ourselves into the character on the screen. 'Identification' can be used to refer to a specially intense relationship of involvement with a particular character but cannot legitimately be extended to suggest the total submersion of our consciousness. A more generally applicable term might be 'association'.

Identification is not necessarily a controlling factor in our reactions. In many comedies our pleasure arises from a relationship of superiority to the characters ridiculously involved in the action of the film. Jerry Lewis has explained the popularity of the idiot-boy personality he presents on film by saying that there can be no one in any audience who does not feel superior to him. The pleasure which much film comedy gives us is in line with Thomas Hobbes's misanthropic definition of laughter as the expression of a 'sudden glory' which 'is caused either by some sudden act of their own, that pleaseth them [identification]; or by the apprehension of some deformed thing in another, by comparison whereof they suddenly applaud themselves [superiority]'.[4] Almost three centuries before it was needed, Hobbes provided a useful distinction between two types of film clown – those whose triumphs we share (the mouse Jerry, Chaplin, Keaton, the Marx Brothers) and those whose humiliations we enjoy: Tom the cat, Stan Laurel, Jerry Lewis, or Peter Sellers as the inept Inspector Clouseau in *The Pink Panther* and *A Shot in the Dark*. But the fluidity of our response is

4. Thomas Hobbes, *Leviathan*, Everyman Library, 1914, p. 27.

noteworthy and must make us suspicious of over-precise definitions. Hobbes's distinction, though real, is unstable: we can pass quickly and smoothly from laughing *at* to laughing *with*. Even Stan and Ollie, those monuments of practised ineptitude, give us moments of petty triumph. Even the dauntless Keaton is from time to time overwhelmed by the world's unreasoning hostility.

A direct relationship with the screen characters offers the surest way of maintaining our involvement. But the fiction film can function without these relationships. We can become involved in the action of a picture in a way which precludes a specific loyalty, a direct emotional commitment to particular characters. Horror films often feed on an obsessive interest in their situations which allows us to enter into the event without caring much about the personalities. The spectator's involvement is a hopeful dread, both wishing and fearing to be brought face to face with the worst thing in the world.

Emotional reactions may be strongly invoked but intellect and judgement are never completely submerged. The subconscious does not take complete charge of the film-dream as it does of the real one. Part of our mind remains unengaged in the fantasy. We know that the experience is unreal and in an important sense unimportant. We are freed from the responsibility of acting upon what we see and feel. Consequently, we can trace our reactions with a detachment which is unattainable in dreams and very difficult in any real situation of like intensity. We can analyse our dreams and our real experiences after the event. In the cinema we can observe our involvement while it is taking place. We enter the film situation but it remains separate from ourselves as our own dreams and experiences do not.

The residue of detachment is sufficient for us to appreciate the most important distinction between movie and dream, which is shape. The fact that movies can offer an organized experience, not just an amorphous fantasy of desire or danger, enables them to go far beyond the artificial indulgence of emotion implied by Montagu's drug or Day Lewis's cheap fur. But the film incorporates the spectator and his emotional reactions into its pattern.

Our involvement becomes as much part of the material as plot and gesture, composition and décor. Our experience as well as the action and image is given significant shape. In this process identification is clearly the chief factor. It becomes one of the variables under (though not completely under) the film-maker's control. And it often provides a key to meaning.

In order to discuss critically we have to find ways of defining not only images, actions and interpretations but also the nature of our involvement. The precise manner in which any spectator involves himself in the action of a movie, the nuances of his alignment with the actions and aspirations of particular characters, will necessarily be controlled by his personality and experience. But critical judgement depends on demonstrating the validity of a response, on showing that it is inherent in the logic of the presentation and therefore depends on a predictability of *dominant* responses. Of course the film-maker himself relies on the accuracy of his predictions in order to control the major pattern of our response to his work. Fritz Lang's *M* concerns a child murderer. Commenting on his presentation of the crime Lang said:

If I could show what is most horrible for *me*, it may not be horrible for somebody else. *Everybody* in the audience – even the one who doesn't *dare* allow himself to understand what really happened to that poor child – has a horrible feeling that runs cold over his back. But everybody has a *different* feeling, because everybody *imagines* the most horrible thing that could happen to her. And that is something I could not have achieved by showing only one possibility – say, that he tears open the child, cuts her open. Now, in this way, I force the audience to become a collaborator of mine; by *suggesting* something I achieve a greater impression, a greater involvement than by showing it. ... In *The Big Heat* [also directed by Lang] Glenn Ford sits and plays with his child; the wife goes out to put the car into the garage. Explosion. By not showing it, you first have the shock. What was that? Ford runs out. He cannot even open the car. He sees only catastrophe. Immediately (because they see it through his eyes), the audience feels with him.[5]

We can feel with screen characters, share their hopes, fears,

5. Quoted in Peter Bogdanovich, *Fritz Lang in America*, Studio Vista, 1967, pp. 86–7.

desires and expectations. But the only actions which we can really perform on equal terms with our heroes are those of the eye and ear. Watching and listening are thus of capital importance as means to create or intensify identification. In *Marnie*, a precise alignment of activity between heroine and audience is used in this way to prepare us for the first climax of suspense. Marnie is about to rob her employer's safe. At the end of the day's work she hides in a lavatory cubicle to await the departure of her fellow-employees. The image of Marnie, leaning against the wall and listening, is held for much longer than might seem justified by its apparent content. But that is just the point. The picture is deliberately boring. Once we have seen that Marnie is waiting and listening, there is nothing more for us to look at. Instead we do what she does. We wait. We listen. The longer we listen, the more concentrated and alert our ears become, picking up snatches of distant conversation, predicting the all-clear of total silence. By restricting his heroine to an activity which the audience can share on completely equal terms, Hitchcock involves us more closely with her. We enter into her situation and become to some extent accomplices to her theft.

In making the spectator an accomplice, and not merely a witness, Hitchcock recognizes and exploits the moral ambiguity of the spectator's position as Peeping Tom. Of all his films, *Rear Window* illustrates this point most clearly because there the hero's functions were reduced, for most of the time, to those of the spectator. The role played by James Stewart in the film was similar to the normal role played by the audience in the cinema. As a photographer confined to one room of his flat on account of his broken leg, Stewart was immobilized like us and, like us, isolated physically from the action which he watched. His speculations about the meaning of what he saw and heard through his rear window were, like ours, guided by the search for diversion in fantasy. The events which took place in the flats across the courtyard from his own were formed, like the events on the screen, by his/our desires and expectations. Watching, for him as for us, gave way to involvement. The result, as in all Hitchcock's best work, is deeply ambiguous. Is the film simply an extended device, designed to maximize our involvement by providing a hero whose limitations are closely analagous to our own, and whose behaviour puts us permanently on tenterhooks for fear that his voyeurism may be exposed because his prying is less securely screened than ours? Or is it by intention what it becomes in effect, a comment on the relationship between audience and film, and on a deeper level between thought and action, fantasy and reality?

In *Rope*, Hitchcock achieved a transference of identification in the last third of his film. For the first hour we share the arrogant elation of his young heroes in the sense of superiority attained by having committed the perfect murder. We identify with them so strongly as to be frightened by anything that threatens exposure – like the episode with the dinner-chest. But as their plot begins to fall apart and their crime becomes more likely to be discovered, our loyalty wanes. We begin to identify with a character who was not seen in the film's first thirty minutes, played the role of an amused if inquisitive bystander in the central sequences, but is more and more clearly destined to become the instrument of our former heroes' downfall. Whereas we originally wanted nothing to interfere with the success of the criminals' enterprise, we spend the final half-hour of the film longing for our new hero to expose the murder.

Our defection is aided by movie conventions. 'Crime must not pay' and greater star-power (James Stewart as the 'detective' versus Farley Granger and John Dall as the murderers) combine to win us over to the side of retributive justice. Hitchcock makes us ignore the conventions when they do not serve his purpose. The exhilaration offered by being made parties to a perfect crime induces us to identify with the murderers and temporarily to overlook the consequences which the conventions hold to be inevitable. However, our awareness of the necessary ending is only dormant. Hitchcock can re-awaken it, as it is useful to him, by removing the counter-attraction and taking the 'fun' out of homicide.

This transference of identification is achieved not simply by an exploitation of convention but by a change in the nature of the dramatized situation. The first half of the film is *about* conceal-ment; the second about search and revelation. Our viewpoint is not given solely by the image because what we see is so much a question of what we're looking for. Viewpoint is also a matter of dramatic focus, our awareness of whose story this is and which are the crucial issues. In *Rope* Hitchcock is able to control our involvement by exploiting two situations, each of which is intrinsically compelling, because it has a built-in dramatic resonance to which every spectator will be sensitive. Hitchcock himself claims that our entry into these situations is not dependent upon a general sympathy for the characters involved:

A curious person goes into somebody else's room and begins to search through the drawers. Now, you show the person who lives in that room coming up the stairs. Then you go back to the person who is searching, and the public feels like warning him, 'Be careful, watch out. Someone's coming up the stairs.' Therefore, even if the snooper is not a likeable character, the audience will still feel anxiety for him.[6]

The screen between ourselves and the film's world allows us to enjoy experiences which would be insupportable in reality. We can indulge desires and impulses which we would not allow ourselves outside this privileged area. In Jung's words, 'the cinema ... makes it possible to experience without danger all the excitement, passion and desirousness which must be repressed in a humanitarian ordering of life'.[7] Our involvement is a game as well as a dream: literally, a game of make-believe.

Our sense of dramatic focus may be largely conditioned by the film's definition of its level of 'playfulness'. The nature of our involvement may be given to us by the overtness with which we are invited to play the game. Indeed, many films guide our identification by allowing us to recognize the winning team. The expectation that everything will come out right in the end makes it possible for us to identify with a character through the most disastrously fraught situations.

Regardless of the playfulness of the film, our drive is to hope for the most satisfying resolution that credibility allows. This is especially important in films where the drive is in fact thwarted.

6. François Truffaut, *Hitchcock*, Panther, 1969, p. 79.
7. Quoted in Manvell, *Film*, p. 8.

The final sequence of Blake Edwards's *Days of Wine and Roses* makes us recognize the inability of the hero's wife to overcome her alcoholism. It would not be able to move us so much if our desire for a satisfactory resolution had not encouraged us, against the logic of the story structure and against our knowledge of the heroine's psychology, to hope for a more reassuring conclusion. The conventional background of happy endings may also be important in providing us with a confidence which is not justified by anything in the situation as presented, but which is necessary to the maintenance of dramatic tension. The balance between our experience and the film-maker's statement is necessarily delicate and fragile.

In two pictures written by Budd Schulberg, Elia Kazan attempted to make film work simultaneously as experience and as protest. His failures are as instructive as they are brilliant. *On the Waterfront* and *A Face in the Crowd* both present situations in which a satisfactory resolution would presuppose a revolutionary change in the modes of thought and behaviour of the societies they portray. But in each case the drama is brought to a resolution. In each case the film-maker seems to get the better of the thinker. Coherent thought is sacrificed to the dynamics of narrative.

Both films are about the abuses of power and influence in an under-educated democracy. Both are clearly intended to condemn the complacent individualism and the lack of collective vigilance which allows power to slide into the hands of men who through malice or stupidity are unfit to lead. Both constitute to some extent attacks upon the audience. The implied statement is: 'this situation can not change unless *you* change'. The resolutions, however, relieve the audience of the responsibility which the films have tried to establish. In both pictures the political situation is resolved (precariously in theory, emphatically in effect) with a lavish emotional climax. An individual act, inspired by personal, non-political motives of revenge (*Waterfront*) and revulsion (*A Face in the Crowd*) overthrows the chief representative of corrupt power.

Kazan, an extremely intelligent director, was presumably aware of his difficulty. His calculation seems to have been that keeping the personal and political action somewhat out of synchronization would allow him to resolve the personal story and complete the movie's dramatic pattern while leaving the wider political questions open. The calculation is reasonable. But the actual effect is very different. The personal story overwhelms the political morality-play. The humiliation of the neo-fascist villains is too decisive. The continuity of political conflict is carefully emphasized, but on the level of statement, not of experience. So decisive a resolution of the personal conflict ends the story with a finality that obscures Kazan's argument. The emotional dénouement refuses to coexist with a rational dissection of political forces. The question 'What happens next?' cannot be both left open to the spectator and answered in climactic triumph. The sense of continuity is lost in the pleasures of the last-reel showdown.

If a film is to have an open-ended effect it is not sufficient simply to leave questions unresolved. They must be seen and felt to be unresolved. Otherwise, the spectator is likely to see a resolution where none is intended or justified. Robert Hamer's *Kind Hearts and Coronets* used this tendency of the spectator in order to cheat the censor. Its hero, having murdered his way past eight obstacles to a title and an inheritance, is tried for a murder which he did not commit. His acquittal provides the desired but forbidden happy ending. In order that his crimes may not be seen to pay, the hero is made to remember in the movie's last few seconds that he has left the journal of his crimes in his cell. This ending satisfies the censor because reason insists that he will be re-arrested and condemned on his own evidence of multiple homicide. But it also leaves the spectator free to complete the action according to his desires. We do not *see* the discovery of the journal or the hero's arrest. What happens 'after the end' is a matter for conjecture. It is consistent with the ironically amoral tone of the picture, if not with reason, to believe that the hero will get away with it once more.

In order to work, the movie has to call on the spectator's imagination to complete the necessarily partial presentation of the world. What is not explicitly stated or shown will be filled in as much by his needs and wishes as by his reason. While Hamer was able to exploit this freedom of interpretation for his own purposes, other film-makers have found themselves exploited by it.

Antonioni's *La Notte* conducts us through twenty-four hours in the lives of a couple whose marriage is foundering. The film ends with husband and wife making love on a golf-course at day-break. Evidently the director did not intend this to work as the conventional happy ending. Although the husband has made a mass of promises for the future, his wife has insisted, and demonstrated, that their love has died. Apart from the arguable symbolic value of the dawn there is nothing to suggest that their copulation is the prelude to a more stable and satisfying relationship. The images, such of them as the British censor allowed us to see, are open to conflicting interpretations. The dawn could mean a fresh start for the film's protagonists. It could be an ironic comment on the unchanged situation between husband and wife. It could also be there simply because hero and heroine have been up all night. The morning light is mistily diffused, which gives us one, optimistic, reading, but also bleak and cold, which suggests the opposite. The golf-course could signify in the openness of its landscape a break from the automatized, externally regulated lives of city-dwellers: the possibility of rebuilding their relationship 'from the ground up'. But it also supports the view that their love-making is a purely physical liaison, casual if urgent, like the mating of stray dogs.

This algebraic approach to the meaning of his film, whether it leads to a hopeful or depressing reading of the final sequence, is precisely what Antonioni tries to avoid. It would not have been difficult, if he had wanted, to establish that the crisis between his protagonists had led to a renewal or to a breakdown of their relationship. He could have confirmed the latter interpretation simply by ending the film a few minutes earlier, or the former by allowing his characters more tenderness in their love-making. Antonioni is interested in the crisis itself, how it arises and what it reveals, not in how it can be resolved. But the spectator *is* interested in a resolution and is likely to impose his own reading of Antonioni's ambiguities.

By placing this episode at the end of the movie the director invites us to give it a particular significance as a prediction for the future of his characters rather than as a simple indication of possibilities. 'What will happen to this marriage?' has been our main concern throughout the film. If we are not given an answer, we are likely to take one. Most people who enjoy *La Notte* seem to have a definite opinion, or rather feeling, about what 'actually' happens after the end of the picture, and, as a result, whether the conclusion is optimistic or otherwise.

La Notte offers us a choice of interpretations. An effectively open-ended picture, like Otto Preminger's *Anatomy of a Murder*, denies us the possibility of interpretation. Preminger's film concerns a lawyer who undertakes the defence in a murder trial. He secures an acquittal but at the end of the picture is still not certain whether he has been defending an innocent or a guilty man. It is essential to Preminger's purpose that we should not be encouraged to resolve the question. If we were able to decide that the defendant was innocent, the film would tend to suggest only that trial-by-jury is a fine institution for determining truth. If the client's guilt was confirmed, we would be drawn to the opposite conclusion. However, the film is designed to examine the mechanism by which a verdict is reached, not to establish the accuracy or fallibility of the verdict itself. A preoccupation with the correctness of the judgement would distract us from the main subject. We must therefore know only that there is a doubt about the defendant's responsibility.

Preminger has two ways of preventing us from an autonomous resolution of the question. In the first place, the completion of the drama is not threatened on any considerable scale by the irresolution of this issue. The dramatic thread which sustains our attention is the defence lawyer's attempt to secure a favourable verdict. Our primary involvement is with the lawyer, not his client; gratification results from the success of the defence and is not dependent upon our feelings towards the accused. We have nothing to gain by endorsing or rejecting the jury's verdict, except the comfort of certainty. Preminger withholds this comfort partly by maintaining the uncertainty of the central character, who will never know whether he has helped to uphold or to cheat justice, but mainly by placing the issue firmly within the category of the unknowable.

This prevents us from making the sort of prejudiced guess that 'concludes' *La Notte*. *Anatomy of a Murder* could run for a further three hours after the end titles, cover another three years in the life of its hero, and we should still be no nearer the truth of the case. In *La Notte* the 'real ending' is knowable but has been withheld. The picture would need to cover at most another two or three hours in its protagonists' lives in order to resolve the ambiguities of its last sequence. In Preminger's movie the story ends with a major issue unresolved. In Antonioni's the story is abandoned when it has served the director's purpose but before it has satisfied the spectator's requirements.

Because our satisfaction is so directly involved, our experience is the more likely to contradict the film-maker's statement wherever the meaning which he offers is less attractive than the one which we can take. Many film-makers have exploited this contradiction between declared intention and actual effect. Their pictures become elaborate and unscrupulous exercises in self-deception. Perhaps the most notable example is *The Bridge on the River Kwai*. Carl Foreman's dialogue repeatedly advertised its interest in establishing the futility of war, the hollowness of victory. But the picture's emotional dynamics invited us to share in the excitements, tensions and triumphs offered by the action. War was said to be futile and experienced as glorious, victory was said to be empty and felt to be magnificent. The destruction which the movie claimed to condemn formed its most spectacular attraction. The picture kept up a prolonged cry of 'Rape!' while undressing and climbing into bed. The film-maker could congratulate himself on the boldness with which he adopted a disturbing attitude without causing the spectator the slightest discomfort.

The real, that is effective, meaning of a film is contained in the total experience which it provides, not in its declaration of intent. The moral significance of Anthony Mann's *The Far Country* is contained within the spectator's relationship to the hero, played by James Stewart. The picture is a success story in a moral key. Granted the violence of the action, the traditional excitements of the Western, the main tension is between our identification with the Stewart character and our awareness of his shortcomings. *The Far Country* is shaped by our desire to see the hero become a more satisfactory identification-figure, not just attractive and accomplished but admirable as well. The film exploits the ambiguity of our reactions to the lone-wolf hero. We identify with Stewart because he embodies the attractions of a life lived solely in terms of the self, recognizing no external obligations and indifferent to the demands of society. His expertise realizes for us the fantasy of power without responsibility. But once we have identified with him we begin to want more from him. We want (him) to be liked and admired by the other sympathetic characters. Through their reactions, in which we are also involved, we feel on his behalf a need which he denies – for an acceptance which can be won only by submitting to the requirements of others. Our involvement makes the film an argument about the conflict between independence and gregariousness in human nature, and between freedom and obligation in human society.

The plot of Mann's film is the process by which the hero is forced to choose between personal comfort and social responsibility. The meaning is in the process by which the audience 'controls' his choice. Without our involvement *The Far Country* would have a different effect and a less direct meaning. If we were free to watch the action with detachment we would also be free to react according to our customary beliefs and prejudices. We might, for example, endorse Stewart's attitude and deplore his ultimate decision as a victory for conformism. But because our involvement is shaped to make us want his choice, we accept from a wide range of possible attitudes the one proposed by the film. We may quarrel with it afterwards, but by then we have already *lived* the film-maker's point of view.

Otto Preminger, in films like *River of No Return*, *Exodus* and *Advise and Consent*, uses identification to create a less linear form. Instead of shaping the experience through a commitment to a particular hero, Preminger divides our allegiance between several characters whose interests and attitudes are sharply contrasted. By eliciting an equally close involvement in different viewpoints on a single conflict, by refusing to weight the film in favour of any one of their attitudes, Preminger produces a form of detachment-in-involvement. The detachment makes it *our* business to reconcile the conflicts. But our involvement is equally important; without an emotional commitment from the spectator the films would become tediously schematic, a conducted tour of arguable opinions. Preminger makes us *live* the argument. The meaning of his film is in the (relative) flexibility of viewpoint which his method provokes.

The contrast drawn in the previous chapter between Preminger's and Hitchcock's methods of creating significant action may be extended here to reflect differences in their ways of moulding our experience. Hitchcock tends to reduce the emotional focus in order to intensify our involvement in a single experience, to present situations as they are felt by particular characters. In *The Wrong Man*, for example, the greater part of the film is limited to presenting the consciousness of the innocent hero as he is overwhelmed by the anonymous processes of law. By contrast, Preminger's 'additive' method works to create an experience which is complicated by the dispersion of sympathy between characters who see and feel the world in conflicting ways.

But nowhere more than in a discussion of film experience are our definitions matters of degree. In Preminger's *River of No Return*, for example, our desire for compromise between the radically opposed attitudes of hero and heroine is *located* in the equal affection for both of them expressed by the hero's son. Conversely none of Hitchcock's films attempts to confine our consciousness *completely* to the experience of his central figure; dramatic effectiveness even in *The Wrong Man*, and very clearly in *Marnie* and *Rope*, depends on multi-dimensional involvement whereby we watch and share the experience not simply of one character but also of relatively minor figures.

Neither Mann's approach nor Preminger's is uniquely of the cinema. As methods of constructing narrative there is no reason for them to be the special prerogative of the film-maker. Hitchcock's identification effects, on the other hand, often are unique because he exploits the directness of our response in a very individual way. The motive behind our identification, not just the fact of it, is integrated into the structure and meaning of his films. Consider the opening sequence of *Marnie*. It is a characteristically Hitchcockian blend of directness and complexity. The first shot shows us a young woman walking away from the camera along a railway platform. Beneath her arm she carries a travelling-bag, evidently well-filled. Her appearance is ambiguously defined in terms of movie conventions and immediately poses the question: professional virgin or whore? Her clothes are unobtrusively stylish; her walk suggests composure, efficiency and, above all, respectability. But she wears her hair long and very black: it might be dyed, it might be a wig, but it is certainly not natural. The face to match this coiffure would be the over-made-up face of a tart. This first shot does not provoke identification. It gives us nothing to identify with: the woman is presented as a figure, not as a character, and she is doing nothing more extraordinary than (we guess) waiting for a train. In its content and through its emphatic presentation, the shot raises questions central to the film's theme. Its main function, however, is to arrest our attention and make us want to know more about the woman. We know that the bag she carries is particularly significant because the shot started with it in large close-up. In the next few minutes we gain more information, enough to make us want to know more still.

The film cuts to a big close-up of a man bitterly intoning the one word: 'Robbed!' He is ugly, angry, middle-aged and perspiring. He recounts how he employed, without references, the good-looking young woman who has just emptied his safe of ten thousand dollars. We share the amusement of the detectives and the contempt of his secretary in observing Mr Strutt's wanly lustful gestures as he describes Marion Holland's provocative 'respectability' ('always pulling her skirt down over her knees as if they were some national treasure'). We know what he really wanted and we enjoy his impotent rage. Through our reactions to the man we identify with Marion Holland (Marnie, the woman with the bag) in a double sense. Because he is repulsive and a born loser we take sides against him and want Marnie to get away with the theft. Also, the reasons for our dislike take us inside the heroine's mind and motives: Strutt, we feel, is a lecherous old sucker who deserved to be robbed. Now this attitude, though we are not aware of it at the time, duplicates Marnie's own. Robbed of his money, Strutt is symbolically deprived of his manhood. But the symbolism is made ours before it is revealed as Marnie's. The irrational connection between sex and larceny is established in our minds before it is mentioned in the picture. Marnie, we later discover, suffers from the interdependent psychological disorders, frigidity and kleptomania. For the moment we experience in the most direct way Marnie's fantasy of immunity through superior cunning. She believes that her own indifference will always enable her to exploit her sex for her own purposes and to control any response which it provokes. The destruction of this fantasy is the film's major theme.

The method by which it is destroyed is exemplified in the second robbery, which follow's Marnie's concealment in the lavatory. As we have seen, the design and effect of this sequence is primarily to heighten our involvement by making us share the heroine's actions, waiting and listening. But it also prepares us for the robbery by making us concentrate on what we can hear: much of the most telling information in the following sequence is carried on the sound-track. Marnie leaves the office door open while she empties the safe – in order to be able to *hear* any approach and not be taken by surprise. An elderly cleaning woman enters the scene at the back of the outer office and starts mopping the floor. As the old lady moves up the gangway towards the entrance of the inner office the sounds of her mopping grow louder and we watch Marnie to see when she will become aware of her danger. Marnie empties and shuts the safe, and is leaving the inner office when she notices the cleaner. She takes off her shoes in order not to be heard creeping towards the exit staircase. One of her shoes edges out of her coat pocket and falls to the floor with a clatter. The old lady goes on mopping undisturbed. Marnie reaches the staircase and Hitchcock resolves the sequence with one of his most disturbing 'gags': the cleaner's deafness is revealed. The basis of our reaction is undermined, after the event. The suspense is shown to have been gratuitous, and the most keenly felt danger (of being heard) quite illusory. The semi-circular movement of this sequence agitates our emotions to amplify our knowledge of the heroine's character. First we share her danger. Then we are made to realize that the danger is unreal; we are separated from the heroine to reinforce our awareness that the apparent triumph of successful larceny is a retreat from her real needs and torments.

Hitchcock conducts us through the enjoyment and endorsement of his heroine's fantasy towards the realization that it *is* a fantasy, and a dangerous one. In the shape of his film we experience rather than observe Marnie's psychology. In this respect *Marnie* is consistent with the rest of Hitchcock's work. By exploiting and revealing quite dubious motives behind our involvement, Hitchcock uses the form of a dream to question its content.

We can see the *Marnie* pattern of guilty involvement in *Rope*, where we are implicated first in the fantasy of perfect murder and later in the illusory claim to judgement over those who have realized our fantasy. Identification with the murderers and with the detective is traced back to the same source, an unwarranted assumption of intellectual or moral superiority. The common theme in *Rope* and *Marnie*, the dominant theme in Hitchcock's work, is the presence of evil and guilt in our most innocent fantasies. Identification based on a shared illusion of superiority embodies the spectator's *hubris*, which the film will attempt to exorcize. Hitchcock is prevented from offering a simple moral – the Christian notion that guilty desire is as destructive as guilty action – by his recognition that fantasy is at the same time dangerous and essential. In Hitchcock's world, a man's moral and psychological integrity, even his physical existence, is threatened by precisely those desires and illusions which make life tolerable. He can survive only by making the most rigorous and lucid distinction between the world as it is and the world as he would like it to be. The total collapse of this distinction, life destroyed by fantasy, is the subject of two of Hitchcock's finest pictures, *Psycho* and *Vertigo*. But a large part of the significance of these films is *in* the experience which they provide. We can summarize *Marnie*'s content and label some of its themes – dream and reality, fraud and self-deception, guilt and atonement, identity, isolation, and so forth – but this does not define the richness and complexity of the film itself. If it did, the film would be superfluous.

Too great a concentration on what a film 'has to say' implies that the significance of a movie is reducible to the verbal concepts which its action suggests. But films are unlikely to replace speech or writing as the medium for examining and conveying ideas. Moral, political, philosophical and other concepts can attain in words an (at least apparent) clarity and precision which no other medium can rival. The movie's claim to significance lies in its embodiment of tensions, complexities and ambiguities. It has a built-in tendency to favour the communication of vision and experience as against programme.

In Otto Preminger's *Advise and Consent* there is a scene where the leader of the majority in the US senate blocks a motion proposed by an obstreperous member of his own party. He does so in order to further the interests of the President. His method is to win time by making a speech in praise of the American constitution with its delicate balance of power between the executive (the President) and the legislature (the Senate). While he is speaking and under his instructions, one of his colleagues crosses the floor to secure the withdrawal of the inconvenient proposal. The senator's action is designed to overcome the freedom of senatorial decision which his words celebrate. The complexity of the scene comes from the simultaneous sincerity and hypocrisy of his actions. It is clear that the senator believes equally in the truth of his speech and the necessity of his intervention. The meaning of the event is not found separately in either of its aspects but in the contained tension between them, a tension which Preminger maintains in his direction by showing both events on the screen at the same time.

The writer-director Samuel Fuller is a master of the balanced contradiction. His films are built around conflicts which are futile and productive in equal measure. War, in *The Steel Helmet, China Gate*, and *Merrill's Marauders*, is both ordered and chaotic, a disciplined and rational form of insanity which makes men's actions ludicrous and magnificent. Courage and cowardice, reason and madness, selflessness and total dedication to individual survival, are revealed in the same events, the same gestures. A discussion of Fuller's themes must set out to reflect the equilibrium between opposed forces and incompatible 'statements'. In *China Gate* one of the soldiers says, 'This is the life for me, even if I have to die to live it' – an absurd contradiction which we come to understand through our experience of the film. In *Merrill's Marauders* a wordless image summarizes Fuller's attitude by finding coherence in the recognition of its opposite: after a gruelling journey and a savage battle one of the soldiers stumbles exhaustedly to the edge of a stream. There he pauses to place his helmet, ammunition belt and rifle in an orderly pile before slumping forward, face first, into the water. Fuller organizes action so that its conflicts are clearly revealed, but not abolished in favour of a single meaning.

The conflicts here are between exhaustion and energy, reason and instinct, shared discipline and anarchic surrender to personal need. Their tension is revealed in action. But any movie which suppresses overt statement in the interest of tension, involvement and belief runs the risk of being taken only at face value. Disguise tends to be too effective. Films which do not solicit interpretation may be represented as insignificant, not subject to interpretation or incapable of sustaining it.

A position of intellectual detachment may hinder understanding. Detachment in its severest and most inhibited form was counselled by the American Professor Herbert Blumer. Young people, he wrote in *Movies and Conduct*, should be instructed not to involve themselves too deeply in the action of a film or in the problems of its heroes, in order not to lose their critical detachment towards the film itself. They should learn to develop adult discount in order to remain consciously the spectators and to avoid becoming sympathetic participants. [8]

Of course it is possible to cultivate this degree of aloofness, rather as Victorian ladies were said to distract themselves from their husbands' nocturnal attentions by thinking over problems of household management. But one cannot analyse, or understand, an experience which one has refused. The programme at the local Odeon or ABC has often been more intelligently received than that at the Academy or Everyman simply because its audience was less insistent on 'content' and more ready to accept the film on its own terms. To recapture the naïve response of the film-fan is the first step towards intelligent appreciation of most pictures. The

8. Quoted in J. M. L. Peters, *Teaching about the Film*, UNESCO, 1961, p. 14.

ideal spectator is often a close relation of Sterne's ideal reader who 'would be pleased he knows not why and cares not wherefore'. One cannot profitably stop there; but one cannot sensibly begin anywhere else.

8 Direction and Authorship

In the factory-like conditions of film-making the notion of the director as a sole creator, uniquely responsible for a picture's qualities, defects, impact and meaning, must be approached with at least some caution. Because it is a collective enterprise, film-making involves many separate personalities, distinct and sometimes conflicting intentions, varying abilities and imperfect control. A movie cannot be fully and uniquely one man's creation.

In *Limelight* Chaplin combined the functions of writer, director, leading actor and composer. We may assume, for argument's sake, that the editing, photography, set and costume design were carried out precisely according to Chaplin's specifications. He would thus have had the greatest control which could be obtained by anyone setting out to tell a story on film. There is no question, in theory or in fact, that *Limelight* is dominated by Chaplin's personality. But it is not the work of Chaplin alone, nor are its qualities entirely derived from Chaplin's dominating presence. There are always the other actors. No complete assessment of *Limelight* could omit to consider the contributions of Claire Bloom and Buster Keaton, the distinct, if integrated, impact of their personalities and performances. However much and however well Chaplin has used them for his own purpose, these remain individual contributions which help to determine the ultimate effect. Simple distinctions between material and composition, conception and realization, group effort and personal control, become quite inapplicable. They ignore and obscure the complexity of a process in which there is no single material and no single treatment, but a series of materials organized in a series of treatments.

To the movie writer a story is material which must be shaped for screen presentation. The actor's material is a film-script with dialogue and action prescribed for a character. But the character can only be given life through the interaction of the writer's conception with the actor's other material: appearance, voice, gesture, intonation, emphasis. Already we have a complex situation in which a character is moulded by two mechanisms, each certainly controlling and probably modifying the other. However, the character as written and the actor employed become material again in the hands of a director. At this stage the image we see and the sounds we hear in the cinema will be established. The work of writers, actors and designers will again be modified in a treatment determined by the director and his photographer. The actor will be placed in a new relationship not only to the story but also to the décor, the camera and the other actors. Even if the director were to exercise no influence over the actor's work, the choice of lighting, composition, colour and camera position – angle, distance, movement – would certainly affect, and could transform, the impact of all the other contributions. The 'finished' performance, scripted, acted and recorded, is material once more when it reaches the cutting rooms. The editor, through his choice and arrangement of images and sounds, will create new, though not necessarily unforeseen patterns, rhythms and emphases. Thereafter the musical score is added and another series of modifications takes place.

The above account represents nothing more than a schematic, for-demonstration-only, plan of the film-making process. The various functions can be distributed or combined in a wide variety of ways. The plan serves its purpose if it makes it clear that so far from offering a simple material organized in a linear process, a film consists of many materials combined, interpreted and transformed through a chain of decisions, treatments and adjustments which continues from the moment the film is first conceived to the time when the spectator leaves the cinema. In this chain each decision limits the subsequent ones, but is also modified by them: for example, a given passage of dialogue limits the actor, but the effect of the dialogue will depend on the way it is delivered.

On film, as in any impure medium, we do not find one coherent material given stable form. Rather we are offered a variety of materials, disparate in kind and function, brought into relationships which we can hope to find pleasant, beautiful, amusing, surprising, significant and so on. The film-maker's control is over these relationships rather than over the separate elements from which they are constructed. Hence our criteria depend more on an achieved balance than on an inherent purity.

A film may have its own unity, with its relationships coherent and its balance precise. But that the ultimate unity can be entirely foreseen is a dubious proposition: the distance between conception and delivery is so great, and the path between them so tortuous and unpredictable. In this connection there are few assertions so misleading, indeed so unlikely, as Lindgren's that 'when the scriptwriter gives himself up to thought, visualizing the white screen before him, he is in precisely the same position as Cézanne before his canvas'.[1] A film (other, perhaps, than a cartoon which might be a one-man product) cannot be made in the mind and then transferred to celluloid precisely as conceived. One of the prime requirements for a film-maker is flexibility to improvise, and to adjust his conceptions to the ideas and abilities of his co-workers, to the pressures of circumstance, and the concrete nature of the objects photographed.

Yet the belief persists that a good film is necessarily a precise realization of one man's precisely imagined vision. Rotha maintains that 'theoretically, the only possible writer of the film manuscript is the director, who alone is capable of transferring to paper the preconception of the film he is about to make'.[2]

But movies can seldom if ever be the unique expression of a creative spirit so dear to the heart and imagination of the orthodox theorist. The director may work in many ways – as creator, craftsman, interpreter, organizer, communicator, propagandist, technician. But whatever the function he performs and the privileges he enjoys, his status must under normal circumstances be that of an employee. The cost of movie production is so high that only a millionaire could afford to make pictures (other than home movies) simply for his own pleasure. Having done so, he would not long retain his wealth without persuading a huge number of people to

1. Lindgren, *The Art of the Film*, p. 202.
2. Rotha, *The Film Till Now*, p. 347n.

share (and pay for sharing) his enjoyment. Even the distinction between 'popular' cinema and the 'minority' movie is dubious. The most popular film reaches only a minority of the public; the specialized picture requires a very large audience. Even a film society is a commercial venture which needs the steady support of a large audience in order to cover its costs. The difference between the popular and the specialized audiences is the difference between a huge minority and a large one. In order to remain active, the director must be the servant of a great mass of people. There is, however, the difference between service and servility.

The difference seems to be not very well appreciated, since the movies are often condemned *en bloc* for their dependence on so large a body of consumers. As Lindsay noted in 1915, 'the haughty, who scorn the motion pictures . . . think that of course one should not take seriously anything so appealing to the cross-roads taste'.[3] In confirmation Mr Arnheim haughtily tells us that 'the artistic film . . . is produced without regard for the general public'.[4] Rotha in a strangely personal version of movie history adds that:

the producing companies made their great mistake when they decided to cater for the taste of the music-hall patron. . . The cinema lost a public who loved it for itself and what it meant to them. . . In the place of the old filmgoer there arose a new type of audience, a vacant-minded, empty-headed public, who flocked to sensations, who thrilled to sexual vulgarity, and who would go anywhere and pay anything to see indecent situations riskily handled on the screen.[5]

The creative cinema of America, says Dr Manvell, 'was destroyed by the need to please continuously the demands of an international audience of a low quality of emotional understanding'.[6]

The belief that popularity and excellence are incompatible dies hard. It survives in the pejorative undertones of the word 'commercial' and in the equation of significance with solemnity and obscurity. It survives in the blanket condemnation or patronage of whole genres of popular cinema, from Biblical spectacles to horror

3. Lindsay, *The Art of the Moving Picture*, pp. 53–4.
4. Arnheim, *Film as Art*, p. 98.
5. Rotha, op. cit., p. 129.
6. Roger Manvell, *The Penguin Film Review No. 6*, Penguin, 1948, p. 121.

movies, from science fiction pictures to Westerns. It survives, particularly, in the notion that the cinema offers two distinct phenomena, one, important, called art, and the other, trivial, known as entertainment. In its crudest form it amounts to the belief that the quality of a film is inversely proportional to the size of its audience.

Evidently we are here dealing with a prejudice akin to that which holds colour film to be, in itself, less 'serious' than monochrome. Furthermore, the prejudice tends to be self-perpetuating; a man who goes to movies looking for triviality is unlikely to find anything else. It is not part of my purpose to invert this prejudice. I have no wish to claim that a popular picture is necessarily a good one, nor to take the financial losses incurred by an unpopular movie as indicative of failures in imagination or creativity. Simply, I should like the words 'popular' and 'commercial' to be used for their limited descriptive value and to be freed from any implied association with critical judgement.

Yet the development of the cinema has beyond doubt been controlled by the fact that its merchandise is actually expensive and potentially lucrative. Work in any medium will take on some of the characteristics of the audience for whom it is designed.

As soon as one attempts to chart the impact of spectator upon film-maker, to arrive by observation or deduction at a summary of the mass audience's requirements and aversions, one is confounded by the enormous diversity of content and method to be found among even the most popular movies.

They are most readily linked by what they are *not*. None of them makes extensive demands on the spectator's intellect. The dialogue and action of each of them is fully understandable without specialized knowledge of political mechanisms, sociological jargon, philosophical concepts or historical facts. None of them employs a form so radically new as to require a substantial readjustment of the spectator's attitude. There is nothing in plot or presentation to baffle anyone who keeps pace with the developing conventions of mid-century, mid-Atlantic popular culture. Where a particular knowledge is required – then it is part of the common knowledge of common man. The spectator does not have to work for his pleasure.

Movies are consumed as 'entertainment', as a spare-time diversion from everyday life. A man who has come home from work looking forward to an evening out with his wife or girl-friend may not reasonably be expected to opt for the unfamiliar in preference to the undemanding, though this fact is often ignored by journalists whose profession it is to watch films and interpret them and who are often grateful for some convenient obscurity needing a couple of hundred words of clarification.

The movie-goer understands films through a large and growing body of conventions, as we all do, but his conventions are not necessarily those of the *Observer* or Pelican reader. He may be well-read in vampire-lore and totally ignorant of the machinery of the British or American constitutions. References to Wyatt Earp, the Alamo, and the KKK will almost certainly mean more to him than references to Orpheus, the Frondes or the ICA. But the list of generally meaningful references, translatable symbols and accepted conventions is far from static. It evolves continuously through infiltration and obsolescence. For if the mass audience tends to be confused and alienated by what is totally new, it has an equal tendency to despise the totally familiar. The director's problem is thus to stay close enough to the conventions to be comprehensible while deviating from expectations sufficiently to be interesting.

All this means a quite substantial limitation on the range of subjects and styles that, at any given moment, the director can offer with reasonable hope of a popular response. Conventions supply only a framework. The more profound and provocative the director's vision, the more important, financially, it becomes for him to embody it in a readily comprehensible pattern of action. The meaning, in other words, must be absorbed into the form. But that seems to me to be as much a mark of excellence within the fiction movie as it is a condition for economic success.

The action of a popular movie can be followed and enjoyed without the need for sophistication or critical discrimination. But a good picture cannot be appreciated in the same way. If one sees *Psycho* or *Johnny Guitar* or *River of No Return* as 'mere entertainment' then one has seen less than half of what they offer. The question, really, is whether a good movie, which is more than entertainment, need be other than entertaining. The answer seems obvious and, if that were the whole question, one would not doubt that the cinema has gained much more than it has lost through its submission to the general will. George Jean Nathan's 'regular and enthusiastic movie patron . . . upon whom a strain may be placed only at the risk of losing him',[7] would seem to constitute just one of those limitations which, in other forms, the theorist has found so beneficial.

However, that is not the whole question. The director is controlled not by 'what the public wants' but by what the public is *thought* to want. His ultimate employer, the cash customer, may supply a framework. His immediate employer, the financier, has often imposed a strait-jacket. The film industry is largely controlled by men who not only claim to be able to predict a picture's prospects by reference to its ingredients (story, cast, setting, etc.) but who also 'know probably less about the process of making films than the manufacturers of any other consumer product in the world'.[8]

Under these circumstances, the temptation is to play safe and dull, to use only those ingredients which are thought to have proved acceptable, and to veto exactly those departures from convention which keep the conventions fresh and interesting. The more recently developed convention of overt unconventionality can of course be just as inhibiting. There can hardly be a single director who has not been frustrated at some point in his career by the financier's belief in a magic formula. In 1936 John Ford regretted the 'constant battle to do something fresh. First they want you to repeat your last picture. . . . Then they want you to continue whatever vein you succeeded in with the last picture. . . . Another time they want you to knock out something *another* studio's gone and cleaned up with.'[9]

As producer and director of his films Otto Preminger works with

7. Nathan, *Art of the Night*, p. 138.

8. Joseph Losey, *Movie*, No. 6, January 1963, p. 20.

9. John Ford, quoted in Jacobs, *The Rise of the American Film – A Critical History*, p. 485.

a much freer hand. But in order to raise the finance for a picture he has still to submit his projects to outside judgement; 'these people,' he says, 'don't have opinions, they have figures. And these figures become taboos. They don't examine a project . . . they just look at their statistics.'[10]

However little he may be made aware of his position, however successfully the arrangement may work, the director is an employee whenever he is not his own financier. His work, the possibility of realizing his dearest project, is always controlled by the man with the money. This rule applies under any system of production. If the director is not required to conform to another's idea of what the public wants, if profit is not the motive for production, he will have to submit to an opinion about what the public needs, or ought to want. His work must be approved for its ideological or artistic qualities. In all these cases, he needs to satisfy tastes other than, but not necessarily incompatible with, his own.

A director has only to withhold such satisfaction in order to discover the nature of the relationship between economic and creative control. Work belongs to its purchaser, not its producer. The director has no ownership in his creations and ultimately no control over the uses to which they are put. The writer may have to watch while his work is 'improved' (or perhaps improved) by others engaged to supply additional humour to the dialogue or romantic interest to the plot. The actor may be important enough to command transformation of the role he is to take, or he may be powerless to protect his performance from being changed or eliminated in the cutting rooms.

A director whose work displeases his employers may find himself out of his job half-way through the filming. When he has completed the picture, key scenes may be hacked out: Nicholas Ray's *Wind Across the Everglades* was so savaged by the producer's scissors that a father-son relationship (in script and shooting) emerged forcibly (in the version shown) as a homosexual one. Scenes or shots may be added to the film in an effort to change its meaning or soften its impact: Losey's *The Damned* was released

10. Otto Preminger, *Movie*, No. 4, November 1962, p. 19.

with a shot inserted into the climactic scene which lifted the guilt for the murder of a leading character (Viveca Lindfors) away from officialdom – she was to have been mown down by gunfire from a helicopter – and placed it on the shoulders of another character. Sound-tracks may be doctored in a number of ways; a director is seldom consulted about the manner in which his work is dubbed for foreign distribution. Music may be used to transform the effect of a sequence: actions which have been designed to strike us as harsh or ironic may be watered down by a background of blatant musical eyewash.

The hire-and-fire system tends to make each actor and technician interested in the separate impact of his own contribution rather than in the coherence of the final result. One's status in the eyes of the boss can become more important than the excellence of one's pictures. A reputation for being 'troublesome' can arise from an unwillingness to do things the shoddy, familiar or cowardly way. And such a reputation can prejudice a director's chances of continuing to practise his craft.

Moreover the boss is seldom nowadays an individual autocrat, capable of persuasion, concession or enthusiasm. Production is no longer personally supervised by such men as Harry Cohn, Louis B. Mayer, Jesse Lasky, Adolph Zukor and Sam Goldwyn. 'The boss' is now a corporate entity, comprised of a number of executives, each with his job and his personal interests to protect. Such a system must tend to encourage indecision and cowardice. 'The story editor of a big studio,' said Nicholas Ray, 'keeps his job longer if he turns down stories, because then he hasn't made any mistakes.'[11] Losey's experience confirms this:

> The biggest cliché of all time is 'I have to look after my investor's money'. The only honest way in which a producer or executive can look after his investor's money.is make the best and most honest picture he can. But he uses this as an excuse . . . for what he doesn't want to do or hasn't the courage or understanding to do.[12]

Thus Minnelli on his *Two Weeks in Another Town*:

11. Nicholas Ray, *Movie*, No. 9, p. 14.
12. Joseph Losey, *Movie*, No. 6, p. 20.

When it was finished, John Houseman, the producer, and I liked it very much for the kind of story it was; but someone in New York, who is no longer with the company (M-G-M), arbitrarily cut the film in such a way that all the things that explained the action of the principal characters were cut out. As far as I'm concerned the film makes no sense whatever.[13]

Robert Aldrich on *Ten Seconds to Hell*:

I don't think anyone ever read the script before we started the picture. They really thought it was going to be an adventure picture with Martine Carol taking off her clothes once or twice ... So when they came on the scene in Berlin and saw this picture, which was pretty melancholy, they were terribly shocked. It wasn't the kind of film they expected at all. So they over-reacted to what they saw. They chopped it to pieces. I think everybody had a hand in the re-editing.[14]

The writer-director Richard Brooks was asked to insert into *The Blackboard Jungle*, his film about delinquency in a New York school, a scene in which the teacher hero was to remark that his problems with the pupils were nothing compared with those encountered in the Soviet Union. Thus the picture would escape suspicion of having anti-American content. Brooks resisted successfully; but on his version of Tennessee Williams's *Sweet Bird of Youth*:

I had a different ending but they wouldn't let me use it ... M-G-M said 'You can't do that. He came for the girl. He doesn't get the girl.' So they said they'd let me shoot [my ending] after they'd had the preview. And, of course, they never did.[15]

Of *Macao* Joseph von Sternberg remarked: 'Instead of fingers in that pie, half a dozen clowns immersed various parts of their anatomy in it.'[16]

The greater the investment in a movie, the greater become the

13. Vincente Minnelli, *Movie*, No. 10, June 1963, p. 24.
14. Robert Aldrich, *Movie*, No. 8, April 1963, p. 10.
15. Richard Brooks, *Movie*, No. 12, Spring 1965, p. 8.
16. Joseph von Sternberg, *Fun in a Chinese Laundry*, Secker & Warburg 1966, p. 283.

pressures to avoid any form of risk, and the more likely the director becomes to fall victim to executive panic, intrigue or inefficiency. Books have been written about the chaos in which *Cleopatra* was created, a chaos which resulted, not so much from some well-publicized displays of temperament and ill-health, as from a lack of coordination between, and management within, the various departments of the 20th-Century-Fox organization. One's surprise when *Cleopatra* finally emerged was not that the film was in many ways unsatisfactory and incoherent. The amazing thing was that there was actually a movie to show, and that so much of it was intelligent, witty and genuinely glamorous. The rule that managerial feet freeze as budgets ascend has claimed such other notable victims as George Cukor's *A Star Is Born*, Luchino Visconti's *The Leopard*, John Ford's *Cheyenne Autumn*, Sam Peckinpah's *Major Dundee*, and Nicholas Ray's *King of Kings*.

This last can serve as an example of what, one hopes, is the worst that may be inflicted on a picture and its creators. Among the insanities which it suffered were: the insertion of a new character into the script several weeks after filming had begun; the later elimination of that character, in the cutting, together with a key sequence into which he had been introduced; re-recording of the sound-track so as to change the dialogue and bring its delivery into line with M-G-M's concept of 'the traditional religious quietness of Christ'; censorship in relation to the character of Salome which robbed her actions of coherent motivation. *King of Kings*, said Ray, 'was in my opinion atrociously edited. This has nothing to do with the technicians, only with those who do not know that "There is no formula for success, but there *is* a formula for failure and that is to try to please everybody."'[17]

Probably the director's bitterest subjection is not to the taste of his public nor to the occasional ineptitudes of his employers, but to the industrial system, the mechanism of movie finance, production and distribution.

In 1959, Robert Aldrich found himself obliged to start filming *The Angry Hills* with a 'loose, wandering' script because the studio's commitments did not leave time for the necessary over-

17. Nicholas Ray, *Movie*, No. 9, p. 23.

haul. 'You get locked into these situations,' said Aldrich, 'and it's difficult to know what to do about them.'[18]

The defects of the system, the necessity for *a* system and the unavoidable expense of movie production put the director at a great disadvantage when compared with, say, the novelist. He is continually making irreversible decisions, passing points of no return, which the writer does not encounter until his work has been corrected, revised, polished and sent to the printer. The director cannot abandon a work when it is failing to fulfil his expectations: even his least satisfactory work has to go on display. He is not allowed the privilege of failure. He cannot go back to revise his work and eliminate faults of structure, characterization or style. He cannot allow his mood to dictate his hours of work; he has to meet a schedule which is perfectly indifferent to depression, sickness or creative exhaustion. Imagination, perception and intelligence are not enough; he must also be a diplomat, able as occasion demands to persuade, reconcile, dominate, scare and inspire his co-workers. We shall never know how many films have turned out badly not through any fault in their conception but through personal incompatibilities within the production team; or through the need to rush the work in order to meet a commitment; or through financial troubles necessitating drastic changes in production plans; or through simple bad luck with locations, the weather, ill-health, censorship and so on.

As long as we concentrate on the director's working conditions and measure them against some ideal notion of how and why good work is created, so long will it seem impossible for good work to emerge from the 'commercial machine'. Thus Rotha reflected on the alleged imbecility of the American cinema (not of specific American films):

Perhaps it was impossible to produce, let alone conceive any work of real aesthetic value when surrounded by the Hollywood atmosphere of dollars and opportunism, where culture and sincerity seem to be unknown qualities. . . . Sincerity of purpose and surroundings bring out good work. Transfer the painter from his disordered studio into a luxur-

18. Robert Aldrich, *Movie*, No. 8, p. 10.

ious apartment with every new-fangled contrivance to hand and he is at a loss.[19]

This nostalgia for a garret-and-absinthe system of production makes righteous, perhaps envious, indignation a substitute for judgement or understanding. Ultimately it frees the critic from the bother of seeing or thinking about the foredoomed failures.

A knowledge of the film industry's mechanics and structure helps us to understand many things. It explains why many promising projects remain unrealized, why directors are often employed on subjects in which they have little interest, why they must often work in collaboration with people for whose talents they have little respect. In brief, it explains why direction is an activity surrounded by compromise and frustration.

'I've been making films for thirty years,' said Mizoguchi.

> If I look back on all I've done in that time I see nothing but a series of compromises with the capitalists, whom we nowadays call producers, in order to make a film in which I could take pleasure. My only real desire has been to be able to make a film according to my own taste. But I have often been forced to accept a job knowing in advance that it couldn't offer the least chance of success and would mean nothing for me but an absolute failure.[20]

Yet Mizoguchi's best films display a continuity of style in which the highly individual compound of sensuality, elegance, bitterness and vigour is very marked. Through a series of assignments, he was able to create a consistent world, a place of brief pleasures and enduring sadness where moments of tenderness and repose break the action with a suddenness that is itself close to violence.

'The system' can account for some of the director's failures and frustrations. But it does not help us to understand or appreciate his successes. The accepted image of 'Hollywood', graveyard of artistic integrity and creative ambition, is the product of some notable martyrdoms: Von Stroheim, Sternberg, Eisenstein,

19. Rotha, op. cit., p. 78.
20. Kenji Mizoguchi, *Cahiers du Cinéma*, Vol. XX, No. 116, February 1961, p. 15.

Welles. . . . But it does not take account of the large number of
directors who functioned superbly within the commercial framework when it was at its most restricting: Ford, Vidor, Hitchcock,
Preminger, Hawks, Boetticher, Fuller . . .

I have offered a frightening picture of what *may* happen to films
and directors through their involvement with a huge commercial
enterprise. But this needs to be balanced by a recognition that the
commercial system can, often does, work in the director's favour.
If he has the good fortune to want to make pictures on subjects
and in styles which the mass public wants to see, the director need
never be aware of restriction or compromise. Minnelli made most
of his pictures for M-G-M, by reputation the most repressive of the
big companies and the one most insistent on its own 'studio style'.
His *Two Weeks in Another Town* suffered, as we have seen, at the
company's hands; but thirty pictures were produced in fruitful
collaboration to offset that one disaster. Not all the movies were
successful, of course, but the list includes such fine pictures as
*Meet Me in St Louis, Under the Clock, The Pirate, An American in
Paris, Lust for Life, Designing Woman, Gigi, Some Came Running*
and *The Courtship of Eddie's Father*. About his working conditions
Minnelli said:

> Nearly always I have the opportunity of working with the writer
> more or less from the beginning. In cases where the script has not been
> completed, I generally work with the writer for at least five or six weeks.
> In some cases I haven't had that time for giving directions; in that case
> it's been done as we go along. The director usually works with the
> writer in preparing the script. I found it that way in all cases. . . . Cutting
> has never been a problem because I've always worked on it in harmony
> with the producer and the studio. There are compromises, of course,
> but I've always been quite satisfied with the cutting in the end. *Two
> Weeks* was just an arbitrary cutting which was completely wrong. That
> happens to everyone, I find.[21]

Any system claims its own victims. The cinema's industrial set-
up promotes certain sorts of subject and treatment at the expense of
others; it involves a waste of much that is potentially valuable.
Judged by their fruits, other systems are not noticeably better.

21. Minnelli, *Movie*, No. 10, pp. 23–4.

172   Film as Film

John Huston said: 'Some of the worst pictures I've made, I've made since I've had complete freedom.'[22] Creative freedom does not guarantee, nor does industrial production rule out, a good result. In the cinema we are involved with a product, not a system of production. We can reach a judgement without knowing how a film was made.

The movies offer a constant challenge to connoisseurship. The credits supplied at the beginning of a picture are notoriously unreliable. Even when they are accurate they suggest a clearer demarcation of responsibility than exists among most film-makers during most productions. They may lead us to credit the writer with dialogue or action improvised by the director or the performers. Conversely, they may result in our attributing to the director visual effects devised by the designer, photographer or colour consultant. Unless one has watched the planning and making of a picture, it is impossible to know precisely who contributed each idea or effect to the finished movie. We cannot, for example, tell to what extent the editing was foreseen by the director during filming, supervised by him in the cutting rooms, or left to the ingenuity of the man named as editor.

Only external information can tell us whether, and for what reason, the subject of a film was chosen by the men who made it; whether the finished product represents what they *wanted* to do or what they were allowed (perhaps obliged) to do. Intentions and creative processes are invisible. At best we guess them or are given external, often suspect, information about them. We cannot do what Ernest Lindgren asks us to do in forming our judgements: 'Look to the operations of the mind which precede conscious creation'[23] – because there is no single mind to which we can look.

Lindgren gives as an example of total creative control the director Vittorio de Sica and his two films *Bicycle Thieves* and *Umberto D.* Both films were written by Cesare Zavattini, a scenarist who exerted considerable influence over the post-war Italian cinema. They are certainly the best de Sica has directed.

22. John Huston, quoted in James Goode, *The Story of The Misfits*, Bobbs-Merrill, New York, 1963, p. 46.
23. Lindgren, op. cit., p. 202.

But they are *not* what Lindgren demands of the finest film, an 'expression of the experience and vision of a single man'.[24] As much of their impact comes from the situations devised by the writer and from the construction of their scripts as from the director's realization of their scenarios. At the very least Zavattini must be granted his share in the responsibility for these pictures. The fact that Lindgren can illustrate his argument in favour of undivided authorship with two films whose authorship *was* divided is sufficient to undermine his theory.

We can sustain the belief that a good film is necessarily an expression of one man's vision, a communication from the director to his audience, only if we can demonstrate a difference in kind and effect between the personal film and the factory movie. The 'stamp of one predominating creative mind' must be visibly distinct from the stamp of several collaborating creative minds. Provided that a film has its own unity, it seems unimportant whether the unity was evolved through cooperation and compromise within the production team or conceived by one man and imposed on his collaborators.

If the relationships established in a film are significant, it makes no difference to the spectator how they came, or were brought about, or to what extent their significance was intended. A movie has a meaning for the spectator when he is able to interpret its pattern of actions and images. Provided that its relationships are coherently shaped, the film embodies – and can be shown to embody – a consistent meaning which may or may not have been sought, or sincerely felt, by the director.

Jacques Tourneur's *The Night of the Demon* is a striking illustration of this. It presents a story of the occult, drawn from M. R. James's *The Casting of the Runes*, in which a modern scientist is gradually persuaded that his life is endangered by the demonic powers of a black magician. The film employs a whole arsenal of devices – shock effects, grotesque comedy, camera and cutting tricks, ambiguities of character and image. Particularly clever is its exploitation of the spectator's inability to distinguish between truth and convincing lies; we are continually aware that

24. ibid., p. 192.

some of the characters within the film story may be 'acting' but we have no means of confirming or rejecting the suspicion. The film's devices are justified in relation to its effect, or purpose, since they have a consistent tendency. They involve the spectator in the process undergone by the hero, steady undermining of rational scepticism and final reduction to a state of panic in which the reality of occult power is recognized.

We can translate the meaning of the movie in two ways, on the basis of its form and on the basis of our experience. In so far as it succeeds in terrorizing the spectator the movie acts as a demonstration. If the film had been unable to call on reserves of superstitious belief in the powers of darkness it would have been unable to convince and so to scare us. To enter into the experience of the film is to share, however temporarily or playfully, its assumptions.

Even if we watch Tourneur's movie with complete emotional detachment it remains, in its dramatic structure, an assertion of the inadequacy of rational scepticism. We may challenge this argument. There is no denying that it is contained (that is consistently provoked) by the picture. But we cannot know from seeing the film how far its 'message' was intended or how far it was an accidental by-product of other intentions. It may be that *Night of the Demon* was made by men who genuinely believe in the power of Satanism. It may have been designed in agnostic fashion to test the hypothesis that we all, secretly and irrationally, harbour such a belief. Or it may have been created simply to provide its audience with ninety minutes of enjoyable terror, and its metaphysical content used, without sincerity, as a means to this end.

We may regard the last as the most likely explanation. But likelihood is a long way from certainty. The question of intended meaning, of sincerity, is left open by the film. Its effective meaning is all that we can be sure of. And it is all that we need to know. If as connoisseurs we wished to place the picture in the context of Tourneur's work and beliefs it would be important to find out how far *Night of the Demon* embodies a sincere attitude to the occult. But so long as we are concerned, as critics, with the meaning and quality of this particular movie such information remains irrelevant.

The fact that movie production is a collaborative enterprise makes the cinema accident-prone. The interaction between the various personalities and talents engaged in making a film cannot be foreseen. The composition of a film unit, like that of a jazz group, determines the personality of the end product.

This is not a matter simply of 'correct' casting among the various artists and technicians who make a definable contribution to a movie. Two talented designers may produce décors of equal excellence, equally appropriate to the job in hand, yet quite distinct in the sorts of emphasis and suggestion which they evoke. Selecting the production team is like a chemical or culinary experiment. The separate elements/ingredients are known but their impact upon each other is a subject for hopeful speculation rather than certainty.

Out of the confusion of temperaments, ambitions and talents, good things often, and extraordinary things sometimes, come. The meal has frequently proved more satisfying than the recipe would suggest or the chef could expect. Some notable examples: *Pillow Talk, Forbidden Planet, Gypsy, The Manchurian Candidate, North to Alaska, Them!, House of Wax, Foreign Intrigue, The Wonderful Country, Sweet Smell of Success.* It would be hard to establish that any of these shows us 'an artist working at the height of his powers', etc. For the most part, the various functions are performed with intelligence rather than inspiration. These pictures are cleverly written, effectively acted and skilfully filmed. But with the possible exceptions of *North to Alaska* and *Foreign Intrigue* (which are perhaps mainly John Wayne and Robert Mitchum movies) their individuality does not seem to derive from one contribution rather than another.

It is not possible for me to trace the precise 'flavour' of these films in other work by the same writers or directors or actors. Their personalities seem the result of particular combinations of talents. Films are 'accidental' to the extent that they evolve unpredictably under the impact of different, often opposed, personalities. They are also impersonal in so far as their styles and meanings are not derived from one man's conceptions. Individual creative responsibility and artistic control are limited wherever film-making is a group activity; that is, almost always. In expressing and exploring group concerns rather than the private interests of a solitary artist, popular films tap one source of coherence that is independent of 'artistic' self-expression.

There are others, notably the story itself. If the director is successful in his attempt to examine subject through story, theme through action, then significance becomes so deeply embedded in the movie that it seems a by-product of the narrative. Conversely, the intention to make a statement becomes unmistakeable when the message is detached from the dynamic of the movie, tacked on to its structure rather than built into it. In John Schlesinger's *Darling*, for example, there is a scene where the heroine wanders into the library of a posh gaming club. There she reads aloud John of Gaunt's speech in praise of England from *Richard II*. We know that the scene is intended to work as ironic comment simply because it has no other function in the film. It does not advance the plot. It tells us nothing about the characters. The speech could as well have been read by a passing charlady as by the movie's heroine; the effect would have been much the same. We notice the meaning because the scene gives us nothing else to notice. Conversely, by following the logic of a story, setting out to solve its problems and realize its possibilities, making it credible and effective, the director may not create a meaning; but he may allow it to emerge. It seems probable that such good movies as *Them!*, *Panic in the Year Zero*, *House of Wax* and *The Scarface Mob* were films of this sort.

The opening sequence of Don Sharp's otherwise uninteresting *Kiss of the Vampire* provides a very striking example of the way in which a strong situation can generate meanings of its own. We are watching the last moments of a burial service. A small group is gathered in respectful mourning around an open grave. The priest intones the ritual of committal with mechanical fervour. Isolated at some distance from the mumbling mourners, a shabby figure drunkenly observes the scene. As the priest finishes his recital the man approaches the scandalized group, pushes his way through to the graveside, claims the gravedigger's spade and, we suppose, the right to be first in casting earth upon the coffin. Instead, he drives the shaft of the spade through the coffin-lid. From inside the box there comes a scream, and the blood of a 'living' person gathers round the break in the wood. A vampire has been exterminated.

The feebleness of what follows suggests that this sequence was devised as nothing more than a suitably shocking hors-d'oeuvre to yet another saga of the undead. But, efficiently filmed, the scene is so dominated by its basic concept that it becomes something altogether more provocative: consecration versus exorcism, a conflict of rituals holy and unholy, the Christian one recognized, complacent and comforting, the other furtive, demonic, violent but effective. The flatness of the filming itself adds to the effect by putting both rites on the same level. We can accept both as necessary or dismiss both as superstitious, but they are so linked that we cannot endorse one while rejecting the other. The significance of the scene is contained in the tension it poses between 'faith' and 'superstition'. All the spectator needs is an adequate grounding in vampire lore. Without that the sequence would not make sense. It would seem that the coffin had contained a live body and that the scream had come from one of the onlookers. Film reviewers have made us familiar with the notion that a director can transcend the limitations of a genre; here, as quite often in the movies, we see genre transcending the limitations of the director.

This can happen whenever the genre contains within its own evolving 'rules' the possibility of coherent meaning. One example, notable in both number and quality, was the series of Western and adventure films produced in the fifties where the shifting settings of a journey paralleled the moral and psychological development of the characters: *Red River*, *The Big Sky*, *River of No Return*, *The African Queen*, *The Far Country*, *The Naked Spur*, *Legend of the Lost*, and many more. Similarly, any credible gangster film, from *Scarface* and *Public Enemy* to *Pay or Die* and *Underworld U.S.A.*, touches on questions of political philosophy. When it shows the mechanics of gang rule the gangster movie is dealing with the concept of Law, and with the relationship between power and fear. A convincing reconstruction demands a coherent attitude to motives and pressures. Theme and meaning are, in a sense, ready-made.

But a director can also exploit consciously the ambiguities of his medium and the possibilities of his genre. Thus we are unable to tell from the film itself whether the variations on a political theme which emerge from Samuel Fuller's *Underworld U.S.A.* are a by-product of the story or the reason for which the story was created. The moral pattern in *River of No Return* seems too fully developed to have been accidental; yet Preminger talks of the film as an assignment undertaken for strictly contractual reasons. In Preminger's film, and in Fuller's, effect and meaning are quite clear. The source alone is at issue and that can be traced mainly by reference to their other works. Again, *The Servant* is a movie with a rhythm, style and texture of its own. Anyone who had read *The Birthday Party* or *The Caretaker* would recognize it as the work of Harold Pinter. Equally, those familiar with *The Criminal* or *Time Without Pity* would soon detect the hand of Joseph Losey. The signatures of both writer and director are quite evident. In various contexts it may be convenient to treat *The Servant* as a Pinter film directed by Losey, or as a Losey picture written by Pinter. But neither the writing nor the direction is submerged or absorbed in the manner required by the 'solitary man' theories of film. *The Servant* is dominated by the tension between two creative minds, two styles, two personalities and two attitudes. But it is *Losey's* version of the Pinter script; and if we are concerned with film as film it is the realization that must claim our interest and judgement.

Any claims made for direction are of course claims about its possibilities, not rules governing its exercise. However wide or narrow the theoretical limits that we place on the director's function, the actual extent to which his authority is established within those limits must vary with each director's ability and involvement.

The director may be little more than an adviser or a catalyst. Certainly it is one of his most important jobs to stand in the place of the future spectator, to embody in himself the absent audience and so to inspire actors and technicians that they give the clearest and most convincing realization of each character and event. His task as the audience's representative is largely a critical one; but his criticism has to be constructive. He must decide on our behalf what we need to see and how and when we need to see it. He is required not only to say when a particular point is obscure or overstated but also to suggest how it may be made more clearly, more subtly or more effectively. His advisory function already begins to be a creative one.

His other most vital responsibility is that of coordination. Directors are needed precisely because film-making involves so many and such varied kinds of creative decision. If a movie is to have even the most elementary form of unity – that is, one in which the various elements at least do not jar – it is essential that actors, designers and technicians work coherently towards an agreed end. The most obvious method of achieving this result is to put one man in charge of the entire operation. The director is there to ensure that the details of performance and recording are related to the total design. It is through his control over detail that the director may become chiefly responsible for the effect and quality of the completed movie.

His task of organization is, in part, a matter of technique and craftsmanship. As interpreter of the screenwriter's work he is employed to ensure that the actors respect the dynamics of the scenario in the rhythms and tempo with which they play each scene. Through his supervision of the camera team he must achieve a sufficient variety in the images to interest the spectator's eye. At the same time he has to secure images that the editor will be able to assemble into flowing and coherent sequence. As a craftsman he must keep a balance that avoids both monotony and disintegration.

Here again, the work of the interpreting craftsman shades off very quickly into the work of the creator. There can be no clear distinction between supervising the cameraman and creating the images, or between advising the actors and moulding the performances. But unless we consider acting and photography to be the whole process of film-making, the director is still a long way from the total authorship that is often claimed for him.

It is clear that, in outline at least, the shape of a picture is controlled by the construction of its script. Over this the director may have no influence at all. Certainly, the word 'direction' implies no such control. By the time the work of direction begins, plot and dialogue are already established; more or less detailed decisions have been taken on character, casting, motivation and setting. The shape of the film has already been sketched and, with that, some part of its meaning has been determined.

Some producers insist that the director's work should begin and end on the studio floor; that he should have no influence over design, cutting, music or any other process that is independent of the shooting. More usually, a director would expect to work in close contact with the writer, to have a voice in the casting, to be allowed dialogue changes at his own discretion, and to guide the work of the editor and the composer. The most powerful directors are virtually their own screenwriters; it is pure formality (plus union demarcation) that prevents, for example, Hitchcock, Preminger and Hawks from receiving credit as co-authors of their screenplays. A more accurate arrangement would often be the French one whereby the director shares the scenario credit and the writer is named separately as author of the dialogue. Directions' most significant fields of control are also those which make up the smallest area of responsibility that a director can be given: at the very least direction determines how a film is performed and how it is recorded.

Control over performance is control over what happens in the film. This control is clearly incomplete. It is exercised within the limits imposed by the scenario and the cast. The scenario dictates a certain minimum of action essential to the plot mechanism. The director's first task is to make that action convincing, interesting and effective. If the plot demands that hero and heroine meet at a party, there is nothing direction can do about that, however much greater the significance that might be derived from having them meet in an elevator or at a gathering of the local parent-teacher association. The director works within the prescribed situation. But given that he works with enthusiasm, and of course talent, the way that he works is necessarily personal.

It is a commonplace that each of us has his own image of a scene described in a novel; in other words that we each direct the scene differently in our minds. How much more must this apply when the director has to complete the vague images of the mind, the sketched action of a scenario, and to produce the concrete, detailed action of a film image. Even when the director himself thinks that he is merely 'doing the script', his choices of gesture, rhythm and emphasis will reflect his own experience, sympathies and convictions.

In order to make a scene convincing for us, the director has first to convince himself. But what, within the given context, is convincing? Whether the characters move or stand still, look at or away from one another, are close together or widely spaced, speak confidently or with hesitation – these and a host of other detailed decisions are required at every moment. These sorts of detail are to a very small extent controlled by the writing. They are part of the business of direction and, in sum, they are largely responsible for the spectator's attitude to the characters and their actions and so for the mood and effect of the scene. The director begins to be the author of the film from the moment when he finds *his* way to make the details significant as well as credible.

Of course, it is open to the writer to state, in some detail, how he wants the scene played; and the director may well believe that his writer knows best. Similarly, the actors may arrive at their own way of playing it, leaving the director simply to accept or reject their decisions.

At the same time it is important to recognize that the director controls the film as much by what he allows as by what he invents. He has to decide whether to accept the suggestions and demands of his colleagues. That decision is itself positive and creative. The resulting action 'belongs' to the director as much as do the details that he himself suggests. Preminger, by reputation the most autocratic of directors, has said:

I never want to have an actor feel that he is directed. . . . If there are two possibilities and the one that the actor suggests is, in my opinion, a little less effective than the one I could suggest, I let him do it his way because I feel I will get something in exchange. It comes easier; it's more right for him, even if it could be improved. It's like a suit which you've worn for a long time; it's more comfortable, it fits better than a new suit.[25]

With actors, as with scripts, the director is given material which can be used and organized but not transformed at will. The star performers influence what the audience expects and therefore how it reacts. The familiar styles and personalities of such skilled performers as Grant, Mitchum, Wayne, Hepburn and Newman necessarily contribute to the total style of any film in which they appear.

The director who is also a producer can allow for this fact when casting his picture. Among Hitchcock movies distinctions of tone, style and meaning can be drawn between those starring Cary Grant and those with James Stewart in the lead. Hitchcock profits from the different sorts of impact that the two personalities make. Another director, Leo MacCarey, remarked that any film with Cary Grant tends to turn towards comedy because the actor automatically seeks out the humour in a dramatic situation. Hitchcock recognizes this in casting Grant for films (*To Catch a Thief*, *North by Northwest*) whose tones are predominantly light and in which Grant's presence acts as our guarantee that all will turn out well. At the same time, he centres his meaning on the moral weakness of the hero's disengaged attitude. In the Stewart films (*Rope*, *Rear Window*, *Vertigo*) the tone is much darker, reflecting the disturbing ambiguities of the central personality. Stewart's bemused detachment is seen as a mask which thinly disguises a deep and dangerous involvement.

Hitchcock is able to absorb the strong personalities of Grant and Stewart into the textures and meanings of his movies. But Hitchcock has the advantage of control over casting: *Vertigo* would have been a very different film if its obsessed hero had been played by Cary Grant. Where the director joins the production after its casting is complete, the personalities of the actors become part of the given material, like the script, which cannot be altered. A Wayne movie is a Wayne movie. How good a picture it is will depend largely upon the extent to which the 'Big John' image can

25. Preminger, *Movie*, No. 4, November 1962, p. 20.

be made to coexist with, or intensify, the significance of the action.

Here again, the director's job is to exploit and organize imaginatively as often as it is to invent. I do not know of a James Stewart performance which is less than accomplished. But the best Stewart pictures are those in which the direction has managed to integrate the tensions of his (screen) personality, to make them contribute to the total pattern: the Hitchcock pictures, Mann's *The Far Country*, Ford's *Two Rode Together* and Preminger's *Anatomy of a Murder* are some of the most notable examples.

Tackling the same problem from the opposite angle, we can observe the continuity of response that a forceful director can achieve with distinctive personalities in a series of different pictures. Nicholas Ray, for example, has drawn unexpected performances from actors whose names have usually suggested toughness and self-sufficiency. Under Ray's direction, Bogart (*In a Lonely Place*), Mitchum (*The Lusty Men*), Cagney (*Run for Cover*) and Heston (*55 Days at Pekin*) revealed surprising dimensions of uncertainty, tenderness and vulnerability. In these respects Cagney's performance in *Run for Cover* was more consistent with Mitchum's in *The Lusty Men*, and with Ray's work generally, than with the established Cagney image. That is not to say that he ceased to be recognizable as James Cagney. The matter is one of emphasis, not of transformation. The personalities of the real stars are complex enough to reward examination from many viewpoints. We should expect different directors to explore and stress different qualities in the same actor. The task for both director and star is to find an effective way of matching the familiar personality of the actor with the special demands of the role.

The director is the only member of the production team who can see (whose job it is to see) the whole film rather than particular aspects, the interrelationship of the parts rather than the parts as separate tasks. As Max Ophuls expressed it: 'There are as many creators to a film as there are people who work on it. My job as director consists of making out of this choir of people a creator of films.'[26] The director takes charge at the point where the components of the film have been assembled and they await their

26. Max Ophuls, *Cahiers du Cinéma*, No. 81, March 1958, p. 4.

organization into synthesis. From this point those components
are going willy-nilly to enter into relationship. Their interaction
can be mutually enriching, controlled and coherent. Since it will
exist, it is best that it exist to positive effect. Correlation occurs
within the image, between images, and across the film's complete
time-span. Change must take place. But organized, significant
change is development. Actors, designers, writers, photographers
contribute major components of this development; the director is
best placed to design the development itself. Being in charge of
relationships, of synthesis, he is in charge of what makes a film a
film.

Direction can determine which objects and actions are to be
seen as foreground and which as background. By controlling the
balance between the elements, by creating a coherence of
emphasis, it can control the priorities of significance and so shape
the movie's theme. The more closely it is adjusted, the more
intimately personal the balance is likely to become. Density of
interrelationship between parts is both the source of contained
significance and the touchstone of style. Style and meaning are
twin products of synthesis; they do not result from a simple accumulation of independent statements by actors and technicians.

A film may assemble a number of such 'statements' and they
may well be interesting in themselves. To this extent it can usefully
be seen as a group work. But if the film's form embodies a viewpoint, explored in depth and with complexity, it is almost certain
to be the director's. He is in control throughout the period in which
virtually all the significant relationships are defined. He has
possession of the means through which all other contributions
acquire meaning *within* the film.

The director's authority is a matter not of total creation but of
sufficient control. The inadequacies of an actor, an editor or a
composer may inflict more or less brutal damage on work which
ought to have yielded a fine picture. Or, skilled cutters and
musicians can do much to make bad work less noticeably bad. But
they cannot put on to film the close correspondence between
character and design, gesture and image, movement and motive,
which a director has failed to create.

That is part of the reason for resisting the claim that the screen-writer is normally the major source of meaning and quality in good movies. So far from creating a finished work, he offers an outline open to an infinite variety of treatments. It may be so rambling, inconsistent and self-contradictory as to defy redemption. However rich its possibilities may seem, it cannot determine the significance or excellence of the realization. There is no such thing as the movie which 'simply films the script'. Too much is added in the transfer from paper to celluloid. If all that is added yields little of extra significance or complexity, why make or watch the movie?

The case is overstated if we fail to consider the possibility of the screenplay's being so tightly constructed and coherently designed towards particular ends that the director needs only to achieve and coordinate the prescribed effects in order to let the *writer's* meanings come through. Here the writer's creative authority could hardly be denied. But there is no reason to wish to deny it. If we observe the frequency with which precision of style and complexity of meaning are chiefly attributable to the director, we do not thereby claim that direction must always and everywhere be the sole source of any meaning we find in a film and any pleasure it gives us.

Nor do we deny that a lively interaction between members of the film-making team *may* create a composite personality for the movie. I have named some films which attain a rewarding level of quality and significance without betraying a dominant 'signature'. The fluke masterpiece – where the various contributions fall into an intricate reciprocity of meaning without the director's causing them to do so – must remain a possibility. But I do not know of such a film. The 'team-movies' which I cited still seem very worth-while, yet they fall rather short of the best the cinema has offered. The argument is circular, since I recognized them as team products by their common deficiency: a looseness of organization, of relationship between parts, that resulted in a provocative combination of ingredients rather than an indissoluble synthesis.

The most telling argument for a critical belief in the 'director's cinema' is that it has provided the richest base for useful analyses of the styles and meanings of particular films. Yet on theoretical grounds alone, when a movie offers a complex and meaningful interrelation of event, image, idea and feeling, it surely makes sense to think the most likely source a gifted director's full involvement with his materials. At this level of involvement decisions which critics may analyse in relation to total style and meaning may be taken by the director simply because they 'feel right' – they *fit*.

The connoisseurship implicit in a view of the director as author does not demand that we see a great director's failures as masterpieces, although it may make them more interesting than a feebler artist's successes. By seeing the connections between a director's films we can become more sensitive to the pattern within each of them. 'Director's cinema' offers us most clues to the understanding which must precede judgement.

9 The Limits of Criticism

The claims I have advanced for the fiction film depend on our seeing and valuing it as a synthetic process whose conventions allow the creation of forms in which thought and feeling are continually related to our common experience of the world. In this view the impartiality of the camera is continually modified but not overwhelmed by the attitudes of film-maker and audience so that 'fact' becomes concept, object becomes symbol; the abstract is approached through the concrete; the particular takes on wider and deeper significance while retaining the full impact of its particularity. The impersonal record is charged with the tensions of an intimately personal response from both film-maker and audience.

What we see here, as elsewhere, is very much a product of what we look for. Judgement will necessarily be controlled by our criteria. That in no way limits the film-maker's freedom. Critical judgements are as much the critic's property as artistic decisions are the artist's. Only if he wants it to be is the film-maker's liberty restricted by our freedom to define conditions under which we regard his work as valuable.

It is a man's own, and legitimate, decision whether to concern himself with any medium for its own sake. He may decide that his own political, racial, religious or even hygienic objectives are of such overriding importance that he will give his admiration to any picture, regardless of formal integrity, which seems to promote those values. He may have no use for the cinema except as moral propaganda, or as an elaborate light-show. What any of us wants from the movies is his personal affair.

But although we each assign functions, hence criteria, on our own behalf, our decisions need not be arbitrary. It is still open to rational discussion how far the functions we assign are appropriate to the matter in view, and to what extent we are demanding of one medium values which can be more fully supplied by another. If we are to claim an interest in film as film our judgements must respect the framework within which judgement can sensibly operate, by presenting criteria which are capable of being most fully realized by medium and form.

The weakness of much criticism is its insistence on imposing conventions which a movie is clearly not using and criteria which are not applicable to its form. Useful discussion of achievements within the popular cinema, in particular, has been obstructed by an insistence on the value of the films that are not made, and a corresponding insensitivity to the value of the actual product. Intelligent behaviour, sophisticated dialogue, visual elegance, profound investigations of character, sociological accuracy or gestures of compassion are demanded from pictures which quite clearly propose to offer nothing of the sort.

The most destructive version of the process is that in which the film is challenged to reveal instant meaning or to be 'thought-provoking'. The movie-as-visual-code is thus promoted at the expense of the meaningful synthesis. There are two ways in which the value of this synthesis can be approached: naïvely, through an unquestioning acceptance of illusion leading to a submersion in the film's world which allows its tensions to be intensely felt but imperfectly comprehended; critically, through a sophisticated awareness of the film-maker's devices and a conscious imaginative collaboration in the creation of his world in order to appreciate its disciplines and penetrate the significance of its structure. Between these lies the danger zone of pseudo-sophistication, where artifice is seen as falsity, and where fiction is despised or patronized for not being truth. Here critic and viewer impose a scheme of selective approval unrelated to the pattern of the film. It is debatable how far the apparently endemic inadequacies of movie criticism are the cause or effect of the poverty of film theory. Have reviewers habitually subscribed to a cult of the obtrusive, admired the proclaimed intention to communicate as against achieved and integrated significance *because* theorists have valued most the crudest juxtapositions? Or vice-versa? Whatever the answer, it seems beyond dispute that we have long needed a language in which to discuss subtlety. I believe a *synthetic* theory, a theory of balance, coherence and complexity, does carry us towards this goal. It cannot do more. Like an artistic discipline a critical theory provides a basis for excellence and neither a substitute nor a guarantee.

It will serve us only so long as we recognize its limitations, together with those of criticism itself as an activity. A critical theory, for example, may in some ways resemble, but is by no means the same as, an artistic discipline. A theory of film is a theory of film *criticism* not of film *making*. We cannot lay down rules for the creators. If we insist on the concept of balance we do not thereby demand to dictate how or between what elements the balance is to be achieved.

I offered the *Psycho* murder as an example of cinematic excellence, and the *Potemkin* lions as an example of the critically suspect. But that is not because Eisenstein infringed an aesthetic law on the proper content of a movie scene; rather, because his animals were inconsistent with the discipline which he had himself established. Unattached stone lions had no place in a film which undertook to convey ideas and emotions through the presentation of experiences believably undergone by a group of rebel sailors.

It is quite possible that on some intensely personal, private level those lions were seen by Eisenstein as a coherent, even essential, part of his film's pattern. However, that is not relevant to our assessment. We can judge the pattern only as we perceive it. If film-making is, as I've implied, a form of play – a problem-solving game of splendid intricacy and potential profundity – it takes on the nature of a spectator sport rather than a private amusement like doodling as soon as it offers itself for public enjoyment and judgement. Its coherences exist to the extent that they are publicly perceptible.

Criticism itself is a public activity, concerned only with what can be communicated. I may *feel* a picture to be coherent but unless I can explain the nature of its coherence my feeling carries no greater critical weight than my response to the colour of the hero's tie. Though we may enjoy swapping preferences and prejudices among friends, a critical judgement is of value only when it can itself be criticized and tested against others' experience and perceptions.

A theory of criticism is useful, similarly, when it helps us to achieve clarity and consistency in our discussion by providing an agreed language in which to express our perceptions and define our differences. Theory exists in the wake of experience and must remain adjustable to new experience. We cannot usefully construct a theory to aid in the judgement of movies yet to be made, but any theory (and particularly the one I have presented) should be disregarded the moment it is seen to obstruct rather than promote understanding and discourse.

I emphasize this point in part because I have deliberately restricted the field of this inquiry in order to examine sources of value within a particular form. Although I have attempted to encompass a large range of types and achievements within the scope of movie fiction, my criteria will be useful so far as they can be refined and defined progressively until they relate to the methods and qualities of specific pictures. Moreover, my definitions exclude some pictures which are quite evidently fictional. The values I have claimed for *Rope*, say, or for *Johnny Guitar*, cannot be claimed, in the terms of this study, for a picture like Godard's *Les Carabiniers*, where the fictional action attempts neither credibility nor the absorption of personal meaning into a dynamic pattern of action. The degree to which *Les Carabiniers* is to be valued will have to be argued in terms other than those proposed here.

So long as we see the definition of criteria as a means of validating enthusiasm rather than contempt, our standards of judgement will be useful for what they include but will have limited reference. The limits are not destructive but necessary. A positive claim, provided that it is rationally sustained, should be given greater weight than a denial of value. If we fail to perceive functions and qualities it may well be because we are looking for them in inappropriate ways. The corollary is that values which *are* claimed should be argued in the clearest and most positive terms. A failure to discern quality is not a demonstration of its absence, but equally its presence cannot be indicated by the kinds of negative statements which movie reviewers have too frequently invoked in the past decade to solicit approval for films which 'escape the confines of narrative' and so forth. The negative rhetorical question, invoking comparisons with developments in music, painting or the novel to demand of us a reason why the film-maker should not tread the same path, is an evasive device. It frees the critic from the necessity of arguing the value of developments in the medium invoked, and it assumes a direct transferability of methods and values from one medium into another. Since there *are* no rules which the critic is entitled to impose on the film-maker, it is folly to acclaim a movie because it 'breaks' them, and all the more important that criticism present a positive statement of the achievements it claims to have located and a clear definition of the formal discipline which made the achievement possible. It may then contribute to a productive collaboration rather than offer a merely rhetorical elaboration of private responses.

I have said that our only guide to the existence of a perceptible pattern or principle of organization is the fact that it *is* perceived, in terms which allow for rational discussion. But it is common experience that a previously unobserved coherence may become apparent in the course of time or through increased familiarity with a work. If we *come* to perceive the pattern, it was presumably always available for perception. The argument spins away and leaves us continually looking over our shoulders at posterity with judgement in suspense.

Faced with these problems, the temptation is to deny the validity of judgement altogether and to confine criticism to a descriptive role with no claim to be able to evaluate. But this position turns out to be sham. Even description depends upon forms of evaluation which are no less 'subjective' than judgement. A descriptive analysis will need at the least to make claims about the distribution of the film's emphasis; and emphasis is as subjectively perceived, relies as much on a personal response, as judgement.

The only way out of our dilemma is by means of a decision: that we shall at any one time define the perceptible by what we ourselves actually perceive or what can be demonstrated to us by others. We cannot evade the necessity for critical integrity and intellectual honesty in the claims we make; nor can we sustain a refusal to judge those qualities in others. There is no point in becoming paralysed by recognition of our judgement's provisional nature. Critical humility is also required; but that is best defined as a willingness to consider others' arguments. It does not require hesitance in standing by our own judgements so long as they remain defensible. Such diffidence leads straight to a subtle arrogance, the more insidious for being evasive.

We have a duty to ourselves to ensure that our standards are as clear and consistent, as perceptively applied, as we can make them. Individually, we can do no more but we should not do less. One advantage of a criterion based on synthesis is that it allows us to assess a *range* of achievements, degrees of productive tension and relationship. It does not oblige us to see a movie as either a masterpiece or a nonentity. Nor does it drive us to see flaws in a film as evidence of stylistic depravity or human stupidity. I have examined such flaws in order to highlight the achievements of directors who have contrived finer integrations and more provocative syntheses. But what confronts us in the moments quoted from, say, *Moulin Rouge* or *The Loudest Whisper* is not so much a specific kind of cinematic 'badness' as the collapse of the claim for a certain type of excellence. All necessary allowances made for the movie whose exaggerations convey pretentiousness or insincerity, whose contradictions betray dishonesty or self-deception, whose flatness displays disinterest or incompetence, the customary defect of the mediocre film is not the presence of some impermissible conflict but the absence of any special quality. Within the positive criteria suggested, a critical argument which demonstrates coherence must, other things being equal, take precedence over one which does not: the *Potemkin* lions could well be vindicated by an appreciation which showed my case against them to be built on an inadequate reading of Eisenstein's form. I do not believe that my case about *Psycho* is similarly vulnerable. No doubt the murder scene can be shown to offer *more* than I have indicated, but that is another matter. We have to take account of our inability to discuss coherence of detail in anything but a very selective manner. The richer and more dense the pattern we find, the more conscious we shall be that time and space allow us to discuss only some representative parts. We have to be willing to show also why we regard particular flaws as crucial, or particular achievements as typical.

The synthetic theory which I have advanced encourages us to look for coherent patterns of interrelationship. It does not give us means of *proving* the credible integration of pattern and action. Our judgement centres on the degree of meaningful interaction within the elements of the film. But a theory of judgement cannot remove the necessity for judgement. There is a necessary conflict between the activities of the film-maker and the critical spectator in so far as the one strives for synthesis which the other can appreciate only by analysis. Our experience in the cinema, directed and shaped as it may be, is a raw experience which we need to master and whose sense we need not only to feel but also to comprehend.

Index

About the Author

V.F. Perkins was born in Devon in 1936 and went to
Alphington Primary School and Hele's School, Exeter.
He pursued his interest in the cinema and began to publish
film criticism while he was reading Modern History at
Exeter College, Oxford. Subsequently he was a
founder-member of the editorial board of *Movie*. He has
contributed essays to books on Jean-Luc Godard and
Samuel Fuller, has been a 'reader' for M-G-M, and has
written scripts for a series of B B C Schools TV
programmes on the cinema, as well as an (unfilmed)
screenplay in collaboration with the director Nicholas
Ray. He taught in London schools and lectured at
Hornsey College of Art before working as a teacher
adviser in the British Film Institute's Education
Department. From 1968 to 1978 he was in charge of Film
Studies at Bulmershe College of Education. Since then he
has worked as a lecturer in Film Studies at the University
of Warwick, where he headed the Joint School of Film and
Literature for ten years from its inception in 1979.